P9-BZR-311

And I'm sure should be an inspiration to us all:

Mrs. Parkinson's Law

Osborn

MRS. PARKINSON'S LAW

And Other Studies in Domestic Science

by C. NORTHCOTE PARKINSON

Illustrated with Drawings by Robert C. Osborn

Houghton Mifflin Company · Boston

1968

Also by C. Northcote Parkinson

Parkinson's Law
The Evolution of Political Thought
The Law and the Profits
In-Laws and Outlaws
East and West
A Law Unto Themselves
Left Luggage

For Children

Ponies' Plot

A portion of this book appeared in the
February 1966 issue of *McCall's* Magazine

First Printing c

Library of Congress Catalog Card Number:
68-29551
Printed in the United States of America

for Ann

Preface

EACH DAY the world divides between those who go out to work and those who work at home. In previous books I have written mostly for those who go to the office, and mainly indeed for men. I have discussed, more especially, the problems of administration and committee, of personal advancement and the avoidance of tax. To make belated amends to the rest of mankind, I turn in this book to the problems of the home. Writing largely, but not entirely, for women, I deal here with husbands and wives, with children and guests, with houses and fittings, with cupboards and cars. But while the help I offer to the housewife is, I hope, effective and timely, the title I have chosen is easy to misunderstand. It might be thought, at first glance, that Mrs. Parkinson had written the book or else, perhaps, that the book had been written about her. That I owe everything to her sympathy and help must indeed be obvious, and there is a sense, moreover, in which Mrs. Parkinson's Law (Chapter 7) is based upon her experience. As editor at one time of an agony column in which personal problems were aired and solved, she has exceptional knowledge of the difficulties and crises which arise in the home. It would be wrong, however, to assume that it is her views which are expressed throughout the book.

If it would be wrong to regard this as Mrs. Parkinson's book, it would be a still greater mistake to conclude that the work is autobiographical. For my aim has been to discuss family circumstances which may be thought fairly normal in Britain and the United States. Our own married life began in Singapore, where the problems, entirely different, included a civil war in the background. As for the daily commuter journey which separates the average couple, that has no counterpart in the life of authorship. The problems created by a lecture tour are real enough but they are of little interest to anyone else. The autobiographical element is small, therefore, but my travels have given me the chance to observe. I have also had some useful experience as amateur architect and builder. Using the knowledge thus gained through the years, I have tried to apply to the home the same insights, for what they are worth, which I have already applied to public and business administration. In comparing the typing pool with the kitchen sink, I came to realize that the essential contrast is one between multitude and solitude. The executive works with others but the housewife must nowadays work by herself. Realization of the housewife's plight led me to the discovery of Mrs. Parkinson's Law, first published in *McCall's Magazine*. By studying the domestic background to the problem and by pursuing the logical consequences from the nursery school into the realm of teenology, I have come to write not an essay but a book.

As in the preface to other works, I must express my thanks to many who have given me aid and comfort, and notably to members of my household; as also to Mrs. J. K. Neill who so efficiently typed and retyped the manuscript. I am indebted as ever to my publishers in Britain and the U.S.A., who have been generous with their time and counsel, as again to the illustrator, Mr. Robert Osborn, who adds his brilliance to the final result. As for the person to whom this book is dedicated, I have been at pains to show that the work, despite its title, was written by me. That does not mean, however, that I worked without her aid. While the responsibility must be mine for any errors of analysis or fact, the credit for what is acceptable must be shared with her. That she could herself have written a better book with the same title I do not doubt and it is only the tasks of domesticity which delay her return to authorship. Until that moment comes, she must forgive me, if she will, for taking her name in vain.

C. Northcote Parkinson

Contents

Mrs. Parkinson's Law

CHAPTER ONE

Romance

THE YEARS OF MAN are three score and ten, but the psalmist forgot to add that a man may be married for fifty of those years, and even married to the same woman. A half century of active life is no great time in which to accomplish any great work of creativity, but it is quite long enough for a dialogue with one other human being. Our sources of inspiration, experience, learning, fantasy and humor are apt to be exhausted in fifty years, if not indeed in fifty weeks (or minutes). The time will come when our anecdotes have been told, our compliments paid, our information shared and our views expressed.

Some careers are more interesting, of course, than others. Test pilots and cat burglars have experiences, no doubt, which they can describe. Secret agents must have stories to tell which are only partly spoiled by secrecy. For the average couple, however, life is less eventful, with crises no more dramatic than a quarrel at the office, a bargain at the supermarket, a parking offense or a burst pipe. Had Sherlock Holmes married, he would have proved an irritating husband in most ways if not in all. Considered as a conversationalist, however, he would have been at least potentially entertaining at breakfast.

bien
après
Ingres
FG

"You recall, Watson — I mean, dear — the League of Redheaded Men?"

"But, of course, Sherlock. A mysterious affair indeed. Have you finished with the marmalade?"

"Perhaps I might swap it for the toast? Thank you. . . . Well, I solved that case yesterday. Nothing to it, mind you, but memorable, nevertheless, for one or two unusual features."

Next week it would be the Speckled Band, perhaps, or the Hound of the Baskervilles, and while there might be nothing especially dramatic about these incidents they would at least afford a topic of conversation. Our own lives are apt to be colorless by comparison. An average couple may have enough in common to enjoy perhaps two years of each other's society. By the third year they may come to suspect that the opposite of Polygamy is Monotony. In short, they can be bored to tears.

In contemplating their state of boredom, people are apt to conclude that it is, and has always been, inevitable. The type of marriage into which they have entered is (to them) universal and eternal, with its drawbacks as inherent as its advantages. If they find it hard to sustain, they suspect that this has always been so, and that previous generations were merely more reticent about problems which we now regard as Psychological and fit therefore for common gossip.

Marriage is not as sanctified, however, as that. What we regard as normal is peculiar, in fact, to our country and our age. Elsewhere and at other times, people have had quite different ideas. Solomon was a case in point, with his seven hundred wives and three hundred concubines. That he had anxieties of his own is highly probable, but his problems were not ours. Moslems with four wives (enough to play

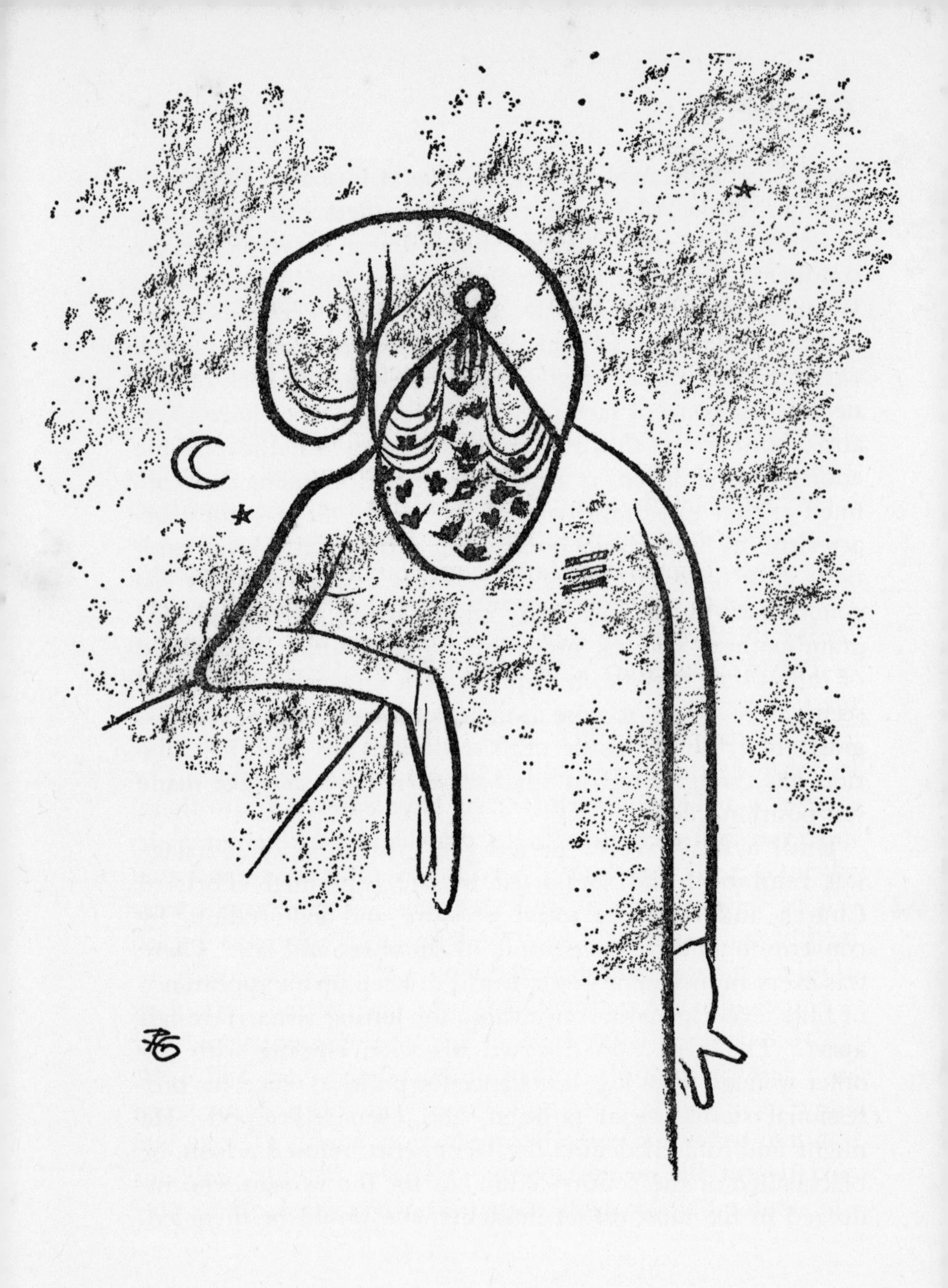

bridge) or Tibetan women with several husbands have worries, no doubt, which are peculiar to them. In their eyes, however, there must be something almost perverted in the conduct of a couple who actually *choose* to live by themselves. What could be less natural? Two people so crazily isolated, without relatives, servants, neighbors or camels — often without so much as a goat — must surely get on each other's nerves? In point of fact, they often do. What we have to realize, however, is that the family of two, with the possible addition of children, is a quite recent experiment and confined at that to certain parts of the world. It was not characteristic of Victorian London, say, where half the inhabitants must have been domestic servants living a more or less communal life as part of a family which often included grandmothers, cousins and aunts. The semidetached world of the suburb may be an improvement on this, but it would seem, at first sight, to pose as many problems as it solves. To grasp the truth of this we need to understand how the situation has changed and in what ways (if any) we have made our position worse.

Until a fairly recent period the institution of marriage was reinforced and supported by the combined efforts of Church and State, by social pressure and exhortation, by convention and by superstition, by snobbery and law. There was every inducement in the world to keep up an appearance of bliss, every penalty conceivable for letting a marriage fall apart. The man who deserted his wife, eloping with another woman, must lose his chance for political office, his professional status, social position, and even self-respect. He might find himself denied the sacraments, refused a loan, or blackballed at the country club. As for the woman who indulged in the most casual infidelity, she would be divorced, disinherited, disgraced and despised. In those days people had every motive for avoiding a scandal, more especially if a man's infidelity were with another man's wife. With the privileges of social position went the duty of sustaining, to the breaking point, a decent appearance of married fidelity. At the lower levels of society the pressures were comparable

and the penalties were, if anything, worse. Until very recently the law has done everything possible to discourage divorce, its concessions being ineffective, reluctant, grudging and late.

When all these pressures were at their heaviest, marriage itself was far easier to maintain. It was, to begin with, of relatively brief duration. Our medieval ancestors married young, the girls often at fourteen, but their lives, on the average, were fairly brief. When anyone reached the age of seventy, it was usually after marrying three or four times. Talk of fidelity "until death do us part" was not as serious a matter then as now. Couples were parted soon enough by famine, plague and pestilence, by childbirth, fire or war. Troth was pledged, in practice, for ten or fifteen years, with remarriage for the survivor. The chances of a marriage lasting for half a century must have been remote. As a sample of sixteenth-century family life we might take *Hamlet,* Act V, Scene II. Before the curtain falls on this everyday scene, the Queen is poisoned, Hamlet and Laertes kill each other, and Hamlet has just time to kill the King before dying. Ophelia's funeral has taken place in Scene I, and we learn now of the execution of Rosencrantz and Gildenstern, making altogether a pretty clean sweep of the original cast. Almost the only person left on the stage is the British Ambassador, looking vaguely for someone to whom he can present his credentials. "The sight is dismal," he remarks, not overstating the case, "and our affairs from England come too late." This we can readily believe, but the fact to observe is the high rate of casualties even in time of peace. Hamlet's wedding, had it taken place, would have been a solemn affair, but his marriage would not have been as momentous an undertaking as its modern equivalent. It could not last forever and it might not, in practice, have lasted for long.

If marriages were once of a shorter duration, they were also less of an exclusive relationship while they lasted. The couple, after the wedding, had relatives and neighbors around them. They were part, as they had always been, of a social and family group, shackled by its conventions, but secure against loneliness. A village was then, as it sometimes is still, a community of related families. So far from ridding you of your relatives, a marriage merely added to their number. As for a great household, there were swarms of servants, constant visitors and repeated occasions for gaiety or grief. Until fairly recently, marriage was diluted by all these other associations. There used to be a stage convention, used by Shakespeare and mocked later by Sheridan, that the heroine had to have a confidante. She was to be followed round by some witless creature to whom everything had to be explained. Even male characters might use a similar device, as in *The Critic,* where Sir Christopher Hatton is made to ask Sir Walter Raleigh, at the outset, why Queen Elizabeth's forces have been mustered.

I cannot but surmise — Forgive, my friend,
If the conjecture's rash — I cannot but
Surmise — the State some danger apprehends . . . .
Sir Walter: Thy fears are just.
Sir Christopher: But where? Whence? When? and what
The danger is — methinks I fain would learn.

This opening gives Sir Walter the chance to explain to his friend (and to the audience) that the Spanish Armada is on the way.

The dumb attendant, as a stage device, was at least based on reality. When Tilburina's friend offers sympathy, she is soon put in her place.

Tilburina: Alas, my gentle Nora,
Thy tender youth as yet hath never mourned
Love's fatal dart. Else wouldst thou know, that when
The soul is sunk in comfortless despair,
It cannot taste of merriment.

"That's certain" is a bystander's unfeeling comment, but

Nora has been useful. More than that, she is to reappear when the tragedy reaches its climax. The stage direction reads, "Enter Tilburina stark mad in white satin and her confidante stark mad in white linen," but Nora is told verbally to keep her madness in the background.

This convention, even when parodied, reflects a society in which people of rank were seldom unattended and even humbler folk were rarely alone. There were always people at hand with whom amazement, annoyance or grief might be shared; people prepared to weep or laugh. The mere fact of marriage did not deprive the gentleman of his valet nor the gentlewoman of her maid. Nor was the valet or maid deprived of other servants with whom the employer's shortcomings might be discussed. There were many drawbacks in life as lived before the year 1900, but the isolation of the individual was not usually one of them. For the psychoanalyst the great days of opportunity were still to come.

While marriage was thus diluted by the presence of other people around, it may be doubted whether medieval husbands and wives expected as much from each other in the first place. They were not as individual as their descendants have since become, and the marriage was not a matter of personal choice. Among families of consequence the premarital negotiations might range from feudal position to real estate, from heraldry to cash. The two persons most affected wanted to avoid a marriage which might prove impoverished or childless, but their personal tastes must have been relatively simple. No great differences of opinion were to be expected in religion or politics, music or food, and the risk of finding oneself married to a total abstainer was negligible. A girl's knowledge of housekeeping might fairly be assumed, as likewise her ignorance of theology or law. A man's status was not a matter of opinion but of fact, his character a matter of common repute, his ancestors known to have been honest or crooked, generous or mean.

In India marriages used to be arranged, through an intermediary, by the parents on either side, the bride and bridegroom meeting for the first time on the day of the wedding. This was never a general practice in the West, but there too it was assumed that marriage was more than a personal affair. The alliance might be made for a variety of reasons, sentiment the least of them, and the parties involved had no cause to complain so long as their partner was suitable in age, rank, health and fortune. In some respects, as for example where property was concerned, our ancestors demanded far more than we do. In matters merely personal, they clearly demanded a great deal less.

Against a general background of marriages planned for practical reasons, there happened, from time to time, a love affair. In the courtly traditions of Provence, a gentleman was almost expected to have a hopeless passion for someone else's wife. If we ignore the troubadours, however (who could be extremely tedious), we still have accounts of other young people who did actually fall in love with each other. Ordered to marry her father's partner, the merchant's daughter eloped with the handsome apprentice. Given a feud between two families of Verona, a son on one side loves a daughter on the other, with grave inconvenience to everyone else. Incidents of this sort did undoubtedly occur and were naturally the subject of general comment, and indeed of disapproval. Lay authority would naturally wish to discourage any conduct which might lead to private warfare, killing affrays and duels. The Church was bound to deplore such passionate relationships as might supplant the love of

God. To idolize a girl is, after all, a form of idolatry. All sensible and responsible opinion was thus in favor of the arranged marriage and utterly opposed to the harebrained love affair.

With all this outspoken condemnation, however, went a lively interest in each elopement, shocked disapproval being mingled with envy. For an escapade rightly described as foolish and wicked might nevertheless, one might imagine, be rather fun at the time. The condemnation was naturally more vocal than the envy, although no one could be blamed for wanting to know all the details before venturing to express an opinion. The most inconsiderate behavior might at least make a good story: a "roman" in French, a tale such as may be found in Greek and Roman literature, pre-Christian in period and terribly pagan in morals. Just such a tale was that of Helen, Paris and the Siege of Troy. Deplorable as it might be in tone — the ancients, after all, knowing no better — there was no denying its value as entertainment. It could even be said to have an eventual moral, for no love affair was ever so utterly disastrous to all concerned and indeed to thousands whose interest was only marginal. The publication of the *Iliad* could almost be justified as an example, to the young, of imprudence reaping its own reward.

The "roman" or romance turned into the novel, a printed account of more (or possibly less) probable events in which a strong love interest is at least usual and almost — dare one say? — invariable. The novelist thus generally preaches the gospel of romantic love. If the hero, the Earl of Normantowers, goes against all better advice in order to marry the pretty daughter of a penniless curate, that is a proper (if not exactly original) subject for romance. Should the same hero change his mind in Chapter XXII, deciding to marry, instead, the heiress to a valuable property in Knightsbridge, that would not be romantic at all. The hero or heroine of romance must thus be prepared to sacrifice all, but all, for love.

This convention is older than the novel, and Jane Austen, the first great English novelist, was prepared to jeer at it. *In Love and Freindship,* which she wrote at the age of seventeen, Jane dealt faithfully with the concept of "love at first sight." In this book she includes all the elements of romantic fiction. The well-born hero rejects the arranged and suitable marriage, quarrels with his father, has adventures and runs into peril, falls in love instantly and is married at once; all as the result of the fiction he has read.

She also anticipates another feature of the romantic novel: the domestic help. The humble cottage in the Vale of Usk, scene of the opening chapter, had servants (plural), and Edward, the unexpected visitor, was not without his groom. Romantic effect would have been entirely spoiled if the heroine had been compelled to wash the dishes. But no eighteenth-century family of gentle birth was ever so impoverished as to be servantless. That is why the most daring innovations of twentieth-century fiction and drama are attributed to "the kitchen sink" school of authorship. With infinite reluctance we have brought the sink into the story, spoiling the atmosphere of romance at the very outset. So far as Jane Austen was concerned, such a development lay in the remote future. Her contemporaries were Romantick, and Sir Walter Scott was more influential than she was. She realized, however, that people are affected by the fiction they read. Novels had already come to be taken as a guide to life.

Since Jane Austen's day, romance has become the accepted

convention. The earlier theories of marriage have gradually weakened, and romantic attachment is now regarded as the central idea. Romantic novels as such have lost something of their influence and might conceivably have died out after their general theme had been exhausted, but romance itself has gained a wider currency than ever before. In the twentieth century the popular newspaper carried fiction to even the poorest homes, and there followed, in rapid succession, the motion picture, the woman's magazine, the illustrated advertisement, the paperback book, radio, pop music and television. The impact of the romantic idea was thus enormously increased and even made visual for the illiterate.

In place of a marriage solemnized by Church and State, by convention and law, we have now the Marriage of Romance. The passionate love affair, once the exception, has now become the rule, no longer discouraged but almost compulsory. Bride and bridegroom are expected to be wildly in love, and people are rather shocked if either admits, privately, that some other motive is predominant. More than that, the romance which sheds a golden light on the wedding ceremony is supposed to continue for life. It is the convention of the novel, as of the fairy story, that bride and bridegroom must live happily ever after. The same assumption underlies the final sequence of the motion picture; as also of the same film when repeated on television. That final and prolonged kiss is the solution, not the posing, of a problem; the end, not the beginning, of the tale.

The weakness of this theory is all too obvious. If we ask so much of marriage and if we depend upon romance as its permanent adhesive, we are all too liable to the penalties of excessive optimism. If we have been properly educated on fiction and drama, we have a vivid idea of the ecstatic mood in which a marriage should begin. The proposal should be made on the mountaintop at sunrise, or possibly on the moonlit boat deck under the tropic sky. The honeymoon should be a time of delirium at Las Vegas or Venice, the first home an adorable cottage in the Cotswolds or Vermont.

But romance, on this level, is difficult to sustain for fifty years. It can, of course, be recaptured, but its rediscovery is apt to be with someone else. And this is where the romantic ideal is weak from the outset. On the theory that love is all, the hero must reject with scorn the prosaic suggestion that he should woo Lady Dorothea or her modern equivalent, the Managing Director's daughter. Instead, he must announce his love for Dolores, the beautiful girl of Gypsy origin whose criminal parents live in the most derelict corner of the flea market. His parents discourage the idea. His elder brother points out the more obvious drawbacks. The Manager tells him that such a marriage will do him no good at the office. The President of the Rotary Club reminds him that other nominations, besides his, have been received. Broad hints are dropped by relatives, colleagues and old classmates at college. All the world is against him; and this is the very situation in which true heroism is revealed. "I love her," he explains simply and the marriage takes place. Seven years later, he is bored to death with Dolores and falls in love with Olga. All his business associates are horrified at the idea of divorce, all his relatives have now accepted Dolores (who has had twins), and everyone agrees that desertion of his family will be at once criminal and foolish. "I love her," he explains, repeating himself, but in a different context, and he is soon married again. The idea that love is all could justify the first marriage, but it can equally justify the divorce; and any future divorce. The question rises as to whether so precarious a relationship is a marriage at all.

At this point a mention of Hollywood becomes inevitable, for the deities of the screen, who have done so much to establish the ideal of romance, have done almost as much to prove its impermanence. Each closing sequence with its Technicolor sunset and celestial choir is a tribute to something which is more a theory than a practice among the screen idols themselves. From here to eternity means about two years and the idea soon prevails that Hollywood morals must be very lax indeed.

The truth is, of course, entirely different. The film star is essentially wedded to the screen, having gained a certain position by dogged perseverance in the most exasperating and tedious career known to man. A married life in the ordinary sense is, of course, out of the question, being incompatible with the hours of publicity and work. To be an old maid or bachelor is equally out of the question as presenting the wrong public image. To be married is therefore essential, and convenient too as a possible answer to importunities from any other direction. But the marriage has never meant, nor was it ever intended to mean, much more than that. And where two film stars marry each other, the chances of their being in the same place at any given time must be remote.

Marriage in this sense is something that the public in general is unlikely to understand. What people do realize is that romance, as dramatized, does not mean permanence. The theory of fidelity, implicit in the motion picture's closing sequence, is thus contradicted at once by newspaper accounts of how the performers actually live. As the chief cement is married life, replacing all previous conventions, romance makes a very poor showing indeed.

Marriages in extreme youth are common and are even defended on the ground that the immature adjust better to each other than do characters already formed, but the objection to them, on the other hand — or at least one objection — is that the early marriage has to last (if it does last) for such a long time. The initial enthusiasm, the romantic impulse, has to be sustained for fifty years. Can any emotion last for as long as that? Among people of any character and intellect, a man does better to marry at thirty, choosing a girl aged twenty-two. The prospects of marriage are improved when something less than the whole life is devoted to it. This is true of marriage considered as a period of years and no less true of marriage as occupying a proportion of the day. The marriage later in life gives people time to have developed interests which will continue; interests in ornithology or Mexico, in poetry or chess. Where these special enthusiasms exist, married couples ask less of each other. Although less dependent, each has more to give. This is a more hopeful situation than one in which they demand from each other what neither has ever possessed.

Is the later marriage really possible? It must be admitted that there are powerful commercial forces ranged against it. Romantic literature and music combine with drama and dance to suggest the urgent need for sexual expression. Morality comes in at this point to discourage sexual activity among the unmarried. There is finally a flood of advertising and salesmanship designed to prove that an early marriage is financially possible, socially desirable, sentimentally attractive and undeniably wise. Some vendors of house property and furniture like to deal with youthful, ignorant and emotional clients. Over every program and from every hoarding shrieks the same message of legitimate sex. Love is all, the advertisers agree, but illicit love is bad for business. Even from the hotelier's point of view, a honeymoon is better than a wild weekend. Best of all, however, is the trade which results from marriage and children, the higher interest loans under guise of purchase on credit, the deals in real estate and the weekly bills for provisions and prescriptions, for diapers and dolls. There are magazines, we know, which cater to the whims of the bachelor or to the man who sees himself as a bachelor for purposes of reading the magazine, but the larger commercial empires have a vested interest in morality. Las Vegas might not be regarded as the most puritanical place in the world but it is, statistically speaking, one of the most religious. The connection between morality and trade is not a theory but a fact.

Romance, as an idea, can be overdone; and we would be still more suspicious of it if we realized that it is a commodity from which other people intend to make a profit. When contemplating marriage, we should, therefore, pay attention to the factors of age, health, family, descent and background, character, courtesy, schooling and brains. There remains, however, at the end, the concept of love. We learn, moreover, from works of fiction that there is a process of being in love which is different in kind from any other relationship. This is a fallacy, but love is certainly important. The practical problem, however, is to decide how much love is necessary and whether it really exists. "I love Mike," says the girl to herself, "but am I *in love* with him?" If she is reasonably warmhearted, she will have loved, in her time, her parents, her younger sisters, her uncle Peter and a number of her classmates at school; not to mention her poodle, two ponies, several kittens and a tortoise. From a study of fiction she concludes that her love for Mike should have reached a further point, should have gone into high gear, in fact, with an audible protest from her emotional transmission.

To listen impatiently for that sort of gear change is a mistake. There is no such sharp distinction, of necessity, between love, as experienced on Tuesday evening and being *in love* as might be the case on Wednesday morning. There is only one kind of love, but it varies in intensity, the point being occasionally reached when a love affair becomes possible. Such an affair involves the coincidence of two distinct emotions. One of these is love, as felt for the poodle or for a school friend, but somewhat heightened. The other is physical desire, as might be felt for a complete stranger. The physical side presents no problem, the presence or lack of the emotion being manifest. But love is a matter of degree, and human beings have no very obvious means of knowing when its boiling point has been reached. How much, they wonder, is enough?

Love is in fact more measurable than many of us realize. It can be measured in terms of human imperfection. Suppose that, for this purpose, a young man's critical eye is apt to compare each girl he meets with an imaginary ideal; a dream goddess called, prosaically, X. He has a certain affection for a dozen girls but is aware, in nearly every case, of a blemish which could or could not be removed. Adèle is pretty but too tall, Betty is amusing but overweight, Carola has a lovely figure but an irritating voice, Diana is a darling but has a bad complexion, Ethel is clever but has no dress sense, Frances is beautiful but inactive, Georgina is popular but spiteful, Helen is attractive but shy. The critical young man may wonder, pensively, whether any of these could be made to approximate X? Could Betty be persuaded to go on a diet? Would Carola agree to undergo speech therapy? Might Diana be fed for a while on lettuces, or Georgina sent to a course in Social Ethics? The answer is that they would, in any case, fall short of X. To be more precise, our young man loves no one of them enough. Why not? Because he can love no one of them sufficiently while he is aware of a defect.

Return, for purposes of comparison, to the dream girl X. She has straight golden hair, candid blue eyes, white skin and a perfect figure. She is intelligent and amusing, considerate and friendly, athletic and kind. Every girl he meets falls short of X in one way or another. Then the day comes when he is introduced to Margaret — a brunette with curly hair, gray eyes, brown skin and of less than average height, more thoughtful than talkative, more perceptive than gay. He thinks Margaret quite wonderful and says as much to his sister. "But Margaret has freckles, which you always detest!" "I know she has, and since meeting her, I have felt sorry for every girl who is *without* freckles." Once he has reached that conclusion, he loves Margaret enough to marry her.

The point is that he loves her as she is, not as she might have been or might possibly become. What is more to the point, she has displaced that imaginary goddess X. Whereas he rejected Betty for not being slim and Georgina for not being kind, he now makes Margaret his standard of perfection by which other girls must be judged. Compared with Margaret, Adèle is taller still and Betty still more buxom, Carola too noisy and Diana too spotty, Ethel too frumpish and Frances too dim. Setting all such comparisons aside, however, no other girl has Margaret's rather gruff voice, no other girl has her powers of observation, no other girl such beautiful hands. Totally unlike X, Margaret is no goddess in any sense. Her qualities are all unexpected, from the quiet companionship of her silence to the quick sunshine of her smile. Margaret's great asset is in being Margaret, and the young man loves her exactly as she is, freckles and all. Given this total acceptance, and given the element of physical desire, the young man may be said to be in love. Does Margaret feel the same? Who will ever know? Let us assume, however, that they marry. This is the point at which the romantic novel ends. In a far more real sense, it is the point at which the real problems begin.

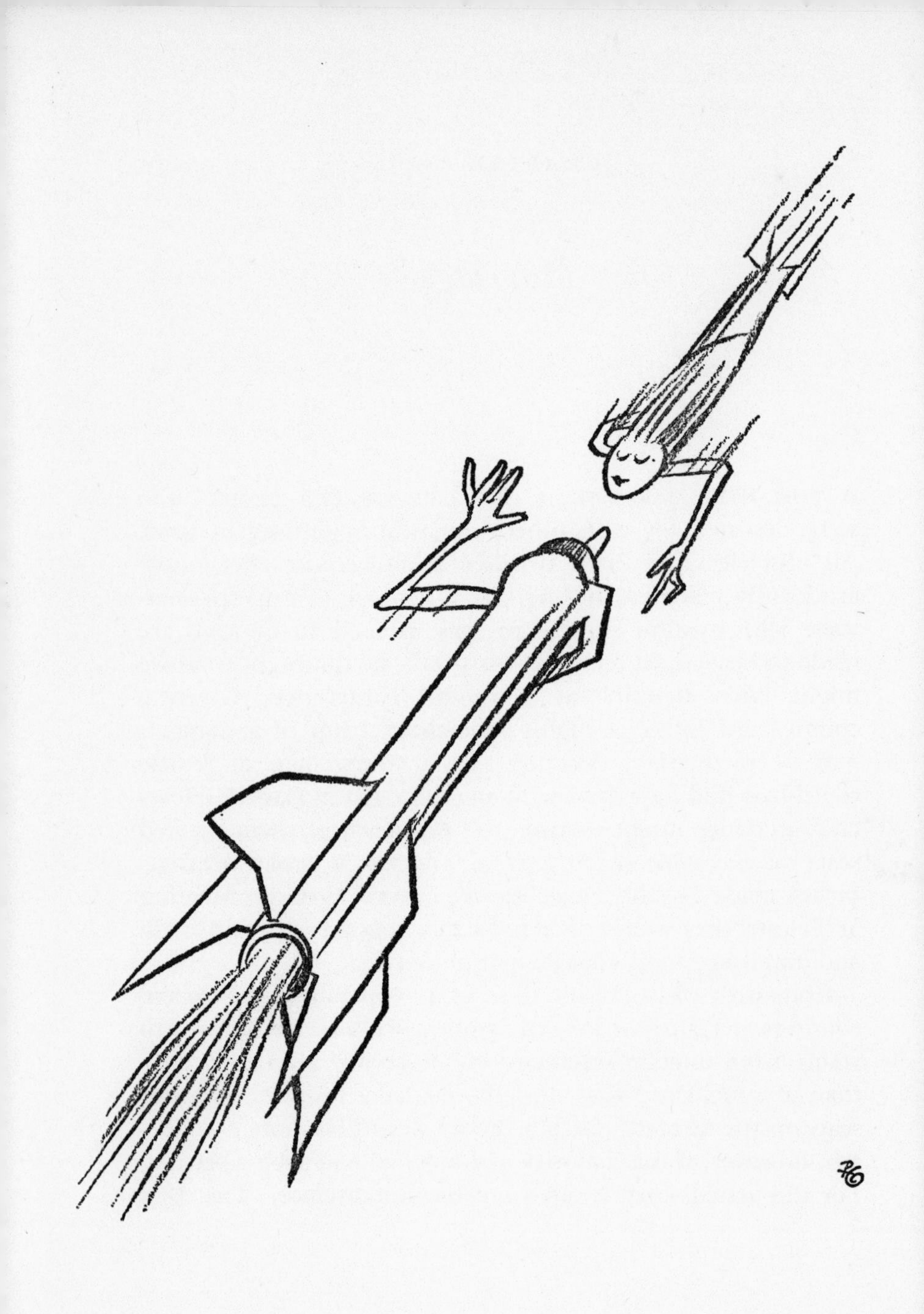

CHAPTER TWO

Marriage

A ROMANTIC MARRIAGE is one between two people who were destined for each other from the beginning of time. All obstacles have been brushed aside because the couple are ideally matched, and neither is capable of a happy marriage with anyone else. Marriages, it used to be said, are made in heaven; in each case the result, no doubt, of what we might fairly describe as a summit conference. Given a cosmic card index, a highly specialized team of archangels may be pictured as deciding that a young man in Seattle could best find happiness with a certain girl in Cardiff. Heavenly guidance might then ensure that each of them booked seats on the same coach tour of Yugoslavia under arrangements made by the Eagerbeaver Travel Agency. Meeting at Trieste, they would dine and dance together at Dubrovnik and announce their engagement at Gatwick.

Romances which result thus from apparently chance encounters at Estoril or Port of Spain might well be thought to result from angelic intervention. It seems, after all, more than a coincidence that they should have reserved adjacent seats on the aircraft! Such a theory would be more convincing, however, if the majority of romances had such a setting. For the actual story is often more commonplace. The Boy meets the Girl in a high school class where each has a total choice (shall we say?) of fifteen. Or the Girl meets the Boy as neighbor in a suburban block where the alternative boys actually number four, one of them a homosexual. Young Man meets Young Lady at College, where the available young ladies number forty-six. Stenographer meets young executive at the office, where the unmarried men number exactly two. By a fairly simple calculation we might discover that the total possibilities for a given person were, say, fifty-one or seventy-eight.

The marriage thus arranged in heaven is based upon a short list made on earth. So far from the archangels flipping over the cards in a celestially limitless filing cabinet, they have actually but a handful of alternatives, all drawn perhaps from the same square mile. Granted that some girls have more young men to choose from, others certainly have fewer. A little research thus reveals that the archangels would have had, in most cases, a relatively easy task; and one best left, in fact, to the girl herself.

The marriage made in heaven is somewhat out of fashion. Its modern equivalent is the marriage arranged by computer. It is theoretically possible for a million bachelors and spinsters to feed into the machine the fullest details of what they have to offer and the fullest description of what they seek to find. Out will come the answer that M/7345162 seems the ideal husband for F/9883694, and she the ideal wife for him. This has actually been done, but not on so large a scale as to have produced any firm conclusion as to its success. Given a sufficiently large number of registered candidates for marriage, the computer certainly offers a scientific approach to the problem. Whether it offers the final answer is another matter. The doubt in one's mind must center, in the first place, on the accuracy of the facts as fed to the machine. The earlier questions in the application form may well be answered correctly, people being fairly truthful about their height, weight, color, religion, education and income; and only mildly misleading, perhaps, about their age.

Beyond a certain point, however, self-portraiture is likely to fail. "Are you a bore?" is a vital question, but how many bores would answer "Yes"? "Are you generous?" might properly be asked, but how many misers would answer "No"? Few people would admit to being quarrelsome, unpopular, idle and dirty. It just so happens (they would explain) that all their neighbors are hostile, their colleagues unfriendly, their employers unreasonable and their water too cold to wash in. Again, few people would describe themselves as snobbish, obstinate, selfish and drab, but all these terms are in use and must apply, presumably, to someone. Least of all will anyone confess to lacking a sense of humor. Far from it! The dreariest of people are ready to see the amusing side of things, but live, worse luck, in a place where nothing funny is said or done. There are reasons, then, for doubting whether the computer will be properly briefed.

People who may be inaccurate about themselves are no more reliable in defining what they want. Gentlemen prefer blondes, it has been said, but marry brunettes; and it is certainly true that the girls they marry may have little resemblance to the girls they have visualized. The young man whose dream it is to marry a redhead, aged 23, 5′7″ high, with perfect figure, athletic tastes, good at languages, fond of music, a Baptist, a Republican, of Scandinavian descent and New England education, will eventually marry a brunette aged 31, 5′0″ high, flat-chested, bookish, with a taste for astronomy and water-colors, an agnostic and Democrat, of Italian origin and brought up in New Mexico. You might think that this change of plan followed the discovery that shapely redheads were unobtainable by anyone in his income bracket. Far from it! The redhead was discoverable, was even available, but had an impossibly irritating laugh. The computer, in other words, might have found what he had asked for without finding what he wanted, raising a doubt in our minds as to whether the thing attempted is even possible. Men seldom know what it is that attracts them. A man will fall in love with A (who rejects him), will nearly cause the divorce of B (who is already married), will have a wild romance with C and will finally marry D. Looking back, he will reflect, perhaps, that these girls were totally unlike each other, physically at least, and that personality, for him, must be all-important. It may be left to his friend to point out that the four girls, resembling each other in no other way, all have an uptilted nose. Only then does he realize — long after the event — that he could not possibly have loved a girl whose nose had curved the other way. This essential fact would be hidden from the computer, because it was unknown, at the time, to the man himself; nor will he know to this day why this one characteristic should attract him.

Admirable in theory, therefore, the computer courtship may be inapplicable to the life we actually have to live; and the idea that two people are destined for each other and that neither could have married anyone else is, of course, an illusion. There might, nevertheless, be no harm, you would think, in people believing that the choice was made in heaven. In point of fact, however, this idea is extremely dangerous. Suppose that a girl begins married life in the belief

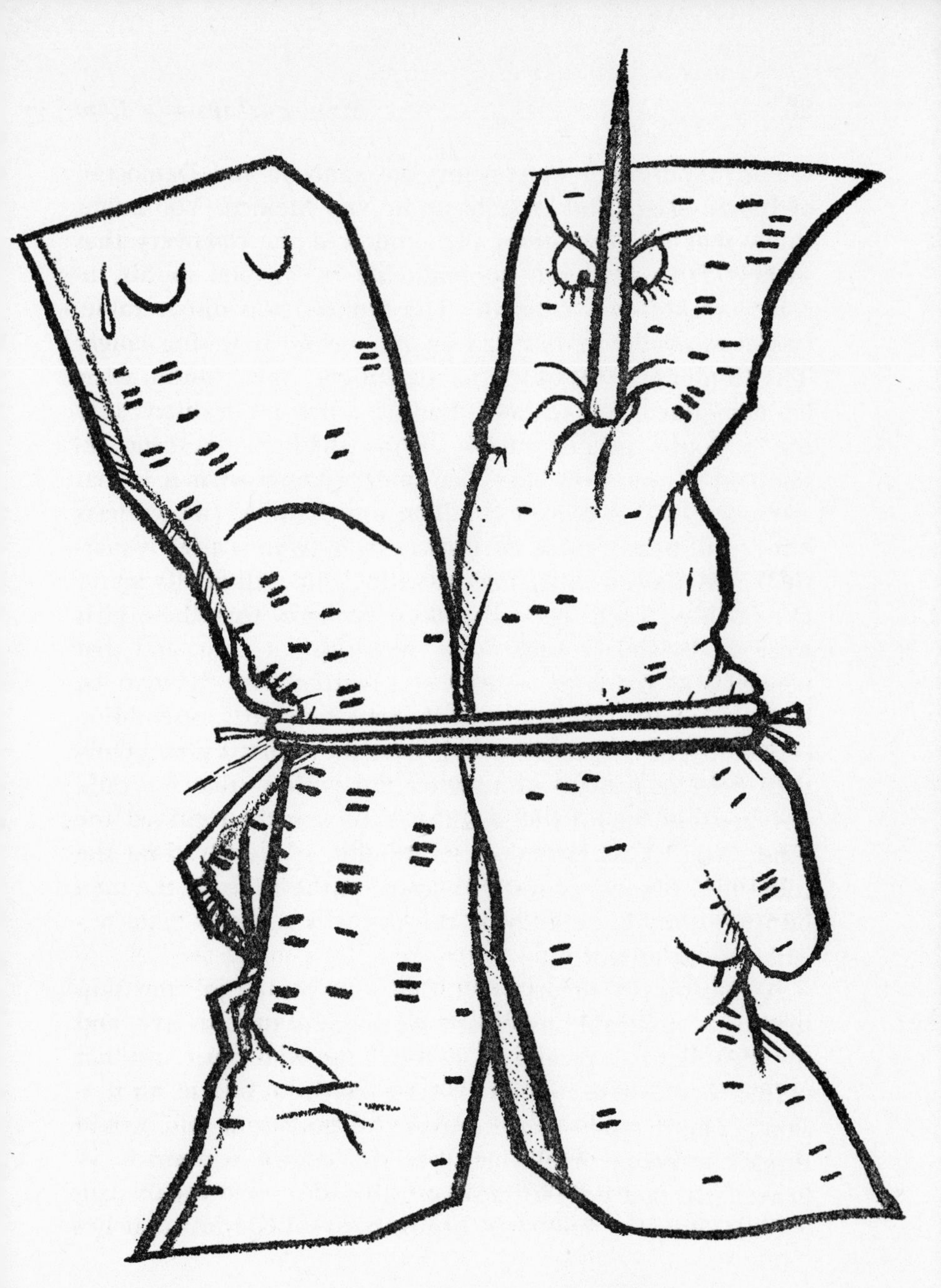
Osborn

that Mike is the only man in the universe she could possibly have married (instead of being merely the best of the three who actually proposed), she may, sooner or later, suspect that the whole thing was based on a clerical error. With all those millions of punch cards, it would have been easy to make a mistake. What if two cards had been stuck together? What if the marriage planned for her with Sorenson, Michael H. (aged 23) had ended, by inadvertence, with her married—quite unsuitably—to Sorenson, Michael M. (aged 31)? This is the sort of thing which happens in even the smoothest organization. The result is that the wife asks herself, "Is this the right marriage? Will it work?" But no marriage will work in that sense. The question she should ask herself is, "How am I going to make it work?" It *has* to succeed, and the only question is "How?"

Marriage is a joint account into which both partners must pay if it is to remain in credit. Its survival turns upon the inherent difficulty of the task, upon the efforts made by each and their success in communication with each other. The central difficulty is the amount of time spent together and, indeed, alone together. It is lessened, obviously, by wider interests, associations, contacts and friends. It is also lessened, however, by the way people develop. Least tedious as companions are people whose interests enlarge and change. Successful are those who can contribute to the joint account from a reserve of unselfishness, imagination, patience and humor. Most successful of all are those who can add a new dimension to the original romance, surrounding crude reality with the golden light of adventure, fiction and drama. But the aspect too often neglected is the art of communication. We express ourselves in words (written or spoken), in gestures or else, sometimes, by silence. Assuming that our

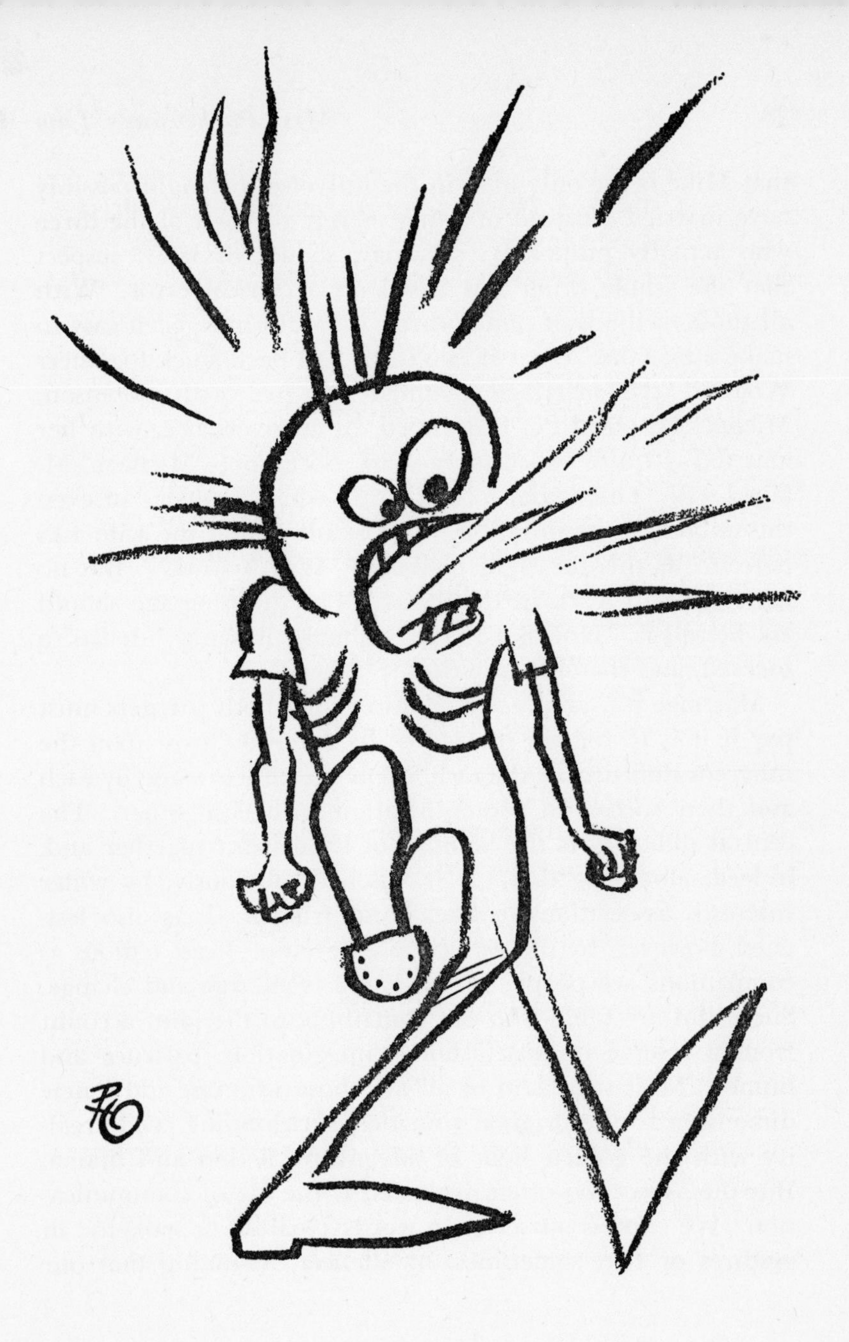

motives are admirable (as we know them to be), we can still produce a crisis by failure to say what we mean; or else, worse, by saying the reverse of what we intend. The whole problem of communication deserves more attention, therefore, than it is usually given.

We have to realize, at the outset, that our self-expression takes two forms: the sort we are born with and the sort we have (possibly) learned. From childhood we have the urge to express our emotions. The baby's wail may have no particular object, being merely the expression of a general annoyance. The child's story of what happened at nursery school is released in a flood of incoherence, not to inform, but merely to relieve the mind of its contents. The man's oath when he drops the hammer has no purpose save to express his irritation. The woman's chatter over the telephone has the effect merely of mitigating her present loneliness. The mind is often bursting with disappointment, with gossip, with envy or joy. Some outlet must be found, and people will often talk to a dog rather than remain silent. The first and primitive aim of conversation is thus to express some emotion we can no longer contain.

The world is full, therefore, of people who speak with no other object than this, falling back on gestures for emphasis and feeling relief when their say has been said. This flushing of the emotions under emotional stress is not intended to explain, instruct, direct or please. At the moment of utterance the speaker is thinking only of himself. All that he conveys is a sense of his weakness under pressure. Whether he can control others is doubtful, for he certainly cannot control himself.

From the age of about five, some of us learn a different form of communication. We begin to speak with the object of conveying a message. We have some actual purpose in mind. Having defined this purpose, we have to make a great effort of imagination. Putting ourselves in the shoes of the person addressed, we have to decide what words are likely to gain the end in view. What does this other person already believe or know? How is he to be informed, impressed or influenced? Starting with the recipient of the message, we work back to the object in view. The form, detail, emphasis and tone of the communication is a reflection of our purpose, not of our current mood. All that we say is deliberate, measured and calm.

Or is it? In practice, we end with a mixture, most of our talk being purposeful but some of it still spontaneous. Opinions may differ, moreover, on the question of which should prevail. Before uttering a sentence the early Quakers are said to have asked themselves, "Is it true? Is it kind? Is it necessary?" If at all dubious, they changed their minds and said nothing. This, within limits, is what we all do, but some people rebel against the conventions, arguing that childlike spontaneity is preferable to an eternal hypocrisy. Why do we not give free expression to all that we think and feel? Why cannot we be honest and say whatever comes into our heads?

The answer is that we are not good enough. If all our thoughts were charitable, kindly, intelligent and pure, there would be no objection to our expressing them. There are people, no doubt, of saintly character and childlike innocence whose thoughts are always fit to share. But few of us answer to that description. Our unguarded remarks, if we uttered them, would be selfish, unsympathetic, irreverent, indecent or harsh.

We have learned, therefore, to suppress our first reactions

and substitute others which we know to be acceptable. Instead of saying what is on our minds, we say what we think will serve our purpose. We adjust our manner to those senior or junior, to those we must instruct or to those we must obey. In casual conversation we seek to entertain or impress, attract or amuse. There will always be some people bursting with something they want to say, and careless of the effect they may have, but these are usually to be classed as bores. The trend in civilized society is toward the deliberate and away from the spontaneous. The only apparent exception to this is among people whose art seems natural. With them all trace of affectation has been set aside, not by a return to the spontaneous, but by so developing the art of courtesy as to make it an aspect of one's being. The chief character in Max Beerbohm's *Happy Hypocrite* wears the mask of a saint but ends by becoming one. Few of us could claim to have done that, but we are all a little more saintly for pretending to be better than we are. At least to some extent, the affectation ends as a fact.

If there is a certain strain involved in our game of pretense, we are tempted to think that marriage will bring with it a sense of release. Our partner will be so close to us that we can revert to childhood, at least in private, and release all that is in us. With one person in the world, we feel, we need have no disguise. In some ways this may be true, but in most ways it is wrong. Living together depends, above all, on courtesy. The affection we have for other people should often make us more than courteous, but it should never, surely, make us less. Kindness goes beyond politeness; it should not fall short of it. And this is the more important if we have children, for their ideas of politeness will derive mainly from example. The courtesy which they offer to others will be a reflection of what they experience at home.

There is no greater mistake than to suppose that marriage frees us from the need to be polite. It rather does the opposite, demanding from us more than politeness in circumstances when our temptation is to offer less. In a play like *Who's Afraid of Virginia Woolf?* we are given a horrifying

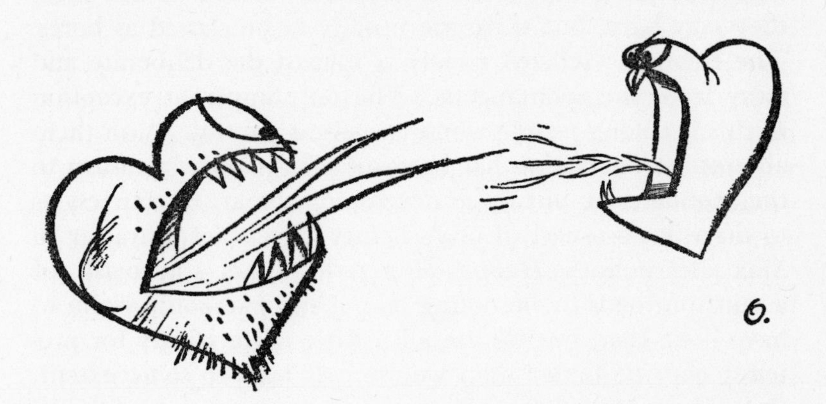

picture of a marriage apparently on the rocks. We realize, finally, that the marriage is to survive but with pain and grief to the two chief characters, as also to their friends and neighbors. The situation is not unfamiliar. What is (we may hope) unusual is the low standard of manners. We are sometimes driven to conclude that what people think may be less important than what they say.

On the subject of courtesy there have always been two schools of thought, the one associated with a more or less deified monarch, the other with the more republican traditions of Greece and Rome. Given a social hierarchy, the forms of politeness are complex, subtle and variable. Such are the problems of precedence that all spontaneous reaction is lost in mental effort. From the Byzantine court we derive such titles as Your Excellency and the forms of address which survive, for example, in Sweden; a country where acquaintances address each other as "Mr. Chief Accountant A" or "Mrs. Assistant Station Master B." Use of the third person, as in answering an invitation, must thus smother the original sentiment in grammatical difficulties.

In eighteenth-century society, where even the most unintentional blunder might result in a duel, the effort to avoid giving offense was understandable and justified. The tradition lingers in the British Parliament, where members must refer to each other by circumlocution and are out of order should they do so incorrectly. "Will the Honourable — no, I mean the Right Honourable — and Gallant — no, Learned Member for Sheffield West — I should have said Sheffield South — agree to withdraw the remark he has just made about the Treasury?" By the time the proper form has been remembered, the original insult has been forgotten. In this way, technicalities have a value, those associated with the court of Louis XIV ending, perhaps modified, as the conventions of Victorian Britain and the United States. Oddest of these, by modern standards, was the custom by which husbands would address their wives as "Madam" and wives would address their husbands as "Mr. Robinson" or "Mr. Smith."

The opposite or republican tradition has often affected the way in which men address each other, and there have always been people who regard politeness as a form of insincerity. It is more honest, they feel, to speak your mind rather than utter meaningless phrases you have been taught. It is a question, however, whether the words spoken in the heat of the moment are not as misleading as the civilities we use to avert open disagreement. Where the choice is between expressing one's momentary feelings and saying what will serve our purpose, the second alternative is usually the better. The effect may be lacking in drama, but it is also, surely, both civilized and sensible.

Behind the forms of courtesy there is the more fundamental problem of who is to lead and who is to follow. Relevant to this question are three characteristics of mankind going back as far as men, recognizable as such, can be traced. Man is carnivorous, first of all, some of his food having always been trapped or pursued, fished or shot. Man is social, in the second place, used to living in a family group or tribe. Last of all, the young of the human species (born singly, as a rule, not in a litter) are helpless for an exceptionally long period, as contrasted with other animals, maturing very slowly and needing protection and care for anything up to twenty years.

Among carnivores with slowly maturing young, there must be a difference of function as between the sexes. With the young to be fed and nursed, protected and taught, the more active pursuits must be left to the male. As hunters at least men have always, therefore, regarded themselves as superior to women. But they have also realized from the outset that the survival of the family group must depend upon keeping the women and children out of danger. If men are killed in hunting or drowned in fishing, the survivors may still be enough for breeding purposes. This cannot be said of the women, upon whose number the natural increase must depend. Men are thus at once superior but expendable, women at once more valuable and subordinate. The basic specialization of the sexes is then given further emphasis by the prolonged differentiation between the adult and the immature. The young of the human species must be protected and taught for so long that their obedience — upon which their mere safety depends — becomes habitual, and remains so, to some extent, after they have reached maturity. In the extended family or tribe, it is essentially the older men who rule, their authority being further emphasized in the special relationship — when it comes to be recognized — of father and child.

So far, then, as nature and tradition are concerned, the man's authority is established. But marriage is a partnership, nevertheless, into which two people have entered for a common purpose, and while there is a sense in which the man's leadership must be assumed, it is clear that the woman's is the bigger investment. She has given up (as he has not) her potential career and freedom. She faces (as he never will) the discomforts, dilemmas and dangers of maternity. Granted that the financial success of the partnership must depend, usually, upon the man's efforts, its failure would bear more heavily upon the wife and mother. Marriage involves, therefore, this central paradox that man, normally the more active partner, is at once superior and subordinate. If he is to be responsible for the family's income, he must have a certain control over the partnership. If he is to do the productive work, he must make the decisions. The executive power is in his hands, and that is where the Christian marriage service puts it. But if the wife is to obey her husband because he is the more active partner, the husband is responsible to the wife because she is the larger shareholder; which makes him, to that extent, her inferior.

As men tend to forget that they hold their power in trust, they remind themselves of it (in some countries) by always treating women as their superior; and it is a mark of our western civilization that they should do so. Men thus rise when a woman enters the room and hold the door open when she leaves. The woman precedes the man in a doorway and is served before him at table. Her wishes are consulted as to where they shall sit or when they will go. There was an element in medieval chivalry which thus made every girl a princess and every man her servant. Underlying it, nevertheless, was the law which made every husband the possessor and every wife a person possessed. From all this we may fairly conclude that the traditional relationship, in Christendom, was one of extreme complexity: the obedience owed by a wife to her husband being nicely balanced by the deference owed to a woman by a man. Far from ending at that point, the niceties of tradition ensured that the formal deference on the one hand should be met by a ladylike hesitation on the other. The girl who was entitled to consideration and compliments was not expected to be opinionated or headstrong. So far as decision making went, she was not to accept more than a part of the power she was ceremonially offered.

In a society where social relationships had become as complex or refined as this, the women suddenly revolted in the name of equality. In the early twentieth century they began to exchange their skirts for trousers. This was, in theory, to demonstrate a new democratic relationship between the sexes. It represented, in later practice, the wartime shortage of men. Women were being employed, and even enlisted, as men, and often used in a role where skirts would have been practically inconvenient or dangerous. The trousers, which were the symbol of defiance, were soon the outward sign of a new servitude, the factory taking the place of the home. With the trousers came the new freedom and comradeship between the sexes. In the brave new world they were to meet at last as equals. Had the revolution been complete, as in some communist countries it would seem to have been, the subtle relationships of tradition would have been wholly supplanted by the arithmetical crudities of the age.

In the English-speaking world there was, however, a compromise. Women were entitled but not compelled to wear trousers. Given the vote, given access to the legislature and to most of the professions, they were also allowed and encouraged to retain the privileges which went with their previous state of subservience. They were allowed to be equal in areas where they had once been submissive, and regarded as superior still in the areas where their superiority had always been acknowledged. In this most subtle of all relationships the earlier sense of balance had been lost.

If a woman is to be treated as a comrade, G. K. Chesterton once pointed out, she is liable to be kicked as a comrade. She will be exposed, in fact, to jeers, curses and horseplay. But such treatment runs so much against all our customary attitudes that we seldom allow logic to take its course. A girl in the army should be treated, in theory, like a private soldier, addressed by her surname and ordered curtly to do this or that. A minute's thought, however, or five minutes' experience is enough to convince any male officer that such a treatment would be lunacy. It may be theoretically correct to say, "Corporal Baker, you are to have these letters ready for signature by midday," but one's actual approach is quite different. "Have you a minute, Valerie? Look, we have to get these done quickly. If you don't want me to face a court-martial, have them finished by twelve. Be a dear and save us all from the firing squad!" This sort of appeal will produce results where the brusque order would gain nothing. All this is perfectly obvious, but it illustrates the way in which the egalitarian theory is practically unworkable. The revolutionary may succeed in abolishing the gentleman, but the woman still wants to be treated as a lady. With the situation thus changed in her favor, she is not always so lady-like as to refrain from using her advantage. In the U.S.A. this is the age of the henpecked husband and the age, in consequence, of the deserted wife.

The realities of the situation are made apparent only when the enlightened folk of the new age choose to visit some more traditional society in which the older values are still upheld. The first instinct of the educated woman is to show a ready sympathy for the downtrodden. "How dreadful!" she exclaims. "Does your husband really order you about? It reminds me of the fairy story about Bluebeard! I never heard of anything so utterly fantastic!"

Gradually, however, she is made to realize that her own example is the subject not of envy but of pity. This is made clear to her by the first local woman she comes to know, whose derision is expressed somewhat as follows: "All your husband says is 'Yes, darling' and 'No, darling' and 'What do *you* think, darling?' Here in Esperanto we like a man who will decide for us and stick to his decision."

"But that is positively *medieval!* My husband and I decide things together without any real disagreement. He is too nice a man to oppose me just for the love of argument, and he will freely acknowledge, if you ask him, that I often know best. Ours is a true partnership, you know, not a tyranny of one over the other."

All this is received, however, with amusement. The women of Esperanto do not regard the "Yes, darling" husband as a man at all. They suspect, to begin with, that he is impotent. When reassured on this point they doubt whether his virility would come up to an acceptable standard. They prefer a man, in short, who behaves like one. Their rejection of the American ideal is outspoken and prompt, and they soon turn from this subject to talk of something else.

Given a normally civilized relationship, the wife has her own way in making about three decisions out of four, two of the choices being probably trivial. Where she most commonly goes wrong is not in demanding her way every time but in openly grasping what she would in any case be given. The lady of tradition saw to it that her husband's final and Napoleonic decision was the result of her previous advice. She prettily yielded to her lord and master, applauding his wisdom and deferring to his deeper knowledge, openly overruled but still aware that the choice was originally her own. The advantages of this maneuver were twofold. In the first place, she gave her husband a sense of dominance without yielding to his foolish ideas. In the second place, she avoided being solely responsible if the decision made were to prove disastrous. It would then have been *his* decision — very natural in the circumstances, mind you, and apparently wise at the time — to which she had innocently yielded without giving the matter too much thought. When the women of today have sufficiently studied the art of marriage, as their grandmothers did, they will come to realize that they can exert more influence by an attractive diffidence than they will ever achieve by militant assertion.

The characteristic mistakes made by the wives of today are partly the result of the female revolt with which this century began but are also the result of their schooling. There is a tendency for girls to receive their instruction mainly from female teachers at school and college who are often (not always) unmarried. So far as their formal education goes, they are thus introduced to life by people whose own ignorance is practically complete. The senior professional career woman is a menace in this context, being a rebel against male exclusiveness and an advocate of sex equality. A wiser and more worldly teacher would assure the girls that any such equality is useless, and that the better policy is to offer an open submission in return for a usually decisive influence. Were but a single school to teach this lesson, the demand for its pupils in marriage would be such as to ensure that the example would spread. It is significant in this context that several of the most exclusive colleges for women have professors who are men. There is something in this idea and it seems preferable, at least, to the plan by which coeducational colleges are staffed (as they sometimes are) by old women of either sex. If there is to be a truce in the sex war, it might come about through women being educated so as to be themselves.

Osborn

CHAPTER THREE

Automotion

We have so far followed romantic tradition as to assume that a marriage should involve, first and foremost, a man and a woman. As a matter, however, of strict chronology, the serpent was well established in the Garden of Eden before the first married couple appeared. The serpent is, of course, a piece of poetic symbolism representing the automobile, and the current Adam must acquire a car before he acquires a wife. To be more precise, he could never, without a car, have acquired the wife at all. While there is a logistic background to this biological fact, we have in it (and more to the point) a subconscious inheritance from the old frontier. The cowboy, that vital factor in American mythology, was inseparable from his horse. Horseless, he ceased to be a cowboy. Without his mustang, he could hardly be said to exist. Mounted, he was something taller than a farmer. Dismounted, he was something less than a child. The horse became the carriage, the carriage became the automobile, and the tradition survives that a man on foot is not even a man.

The classic book on automotion (*The Insolent Chariots*) was written long ago (1958) by John Keats, and there is little that anyone can add. The automobile, he points out, was first produced in the form that we know in 1895. This was

Levassor's Panhard, from which all modern cars derive. Its indifferent design was initially drawn by "a gaggle of village pipefitters" whose amateur plumbing still holds the field. Into the early automotion industry came Mr. Henry Ford and Mr. R. E. Olds, who made Detroit what it is. Cars were mass produced from about 1903, and have since become our

way of life. We are all automotivated, whether we like it or not. It is not a question of choice. We live, rather, in a world in which automotivity is assumed, and in which no other life is really possible. To live in Los Angeles, say, without a car would be scarcely feasible.

Let us suppose, to illustrate this point, that Perry Mason has only a bicycle and that Paul Drake is dependent upon public transport. Della Street answers the phone and tells Perry that his client, Frank Wittering (wrongly accused of murder and now on the run), is at the Disneyland Motel, but that his girl friend, Diana Dithers, is about to commit suicide at an address in Pasadena. "Help is at hand," Perry tells them. "Do nothing until you see me or Mr. Drake." Hanging up, he announces that there is not a moment to lose. He *must* talk to Frank before the District Attorney catches up with him. "And you, Paul, get hold of this girl before she puts her head in the gas oven."

"Okay, Perry," says Paul. "But how am I going to get there?"

"Leave it to Della," says Perry, and goes off to get his bicycle.

Della is, of course, a mine of information, timetable in hand. "There is a bus which stops just two blocks from here and would get you part of the way. You have just missed one and the next will be in fifty-five minutes' time. At Glendale you can get another bus to San Marino — that is, if it runs on Saturdays. This girl's address is really halfway between Pasadena and Sierra Madre and about four miles from either."

"Is there a bus from San Marino?"

"I guess not. Seems like you'll have to walk."

Perry, more fortunate, is delayed only by the need to inflate his rear tire. Then he is off at full speed, with barely sixty-five miles to cover. He would have made it, too, had he not walked up that hill near Buena Park. Being arrested for loitering, he wasted two hours in explanation and reached the Disneyland Motel after sunset. Frank is already in jail and Perry is arrested again, this time for having no lamp on his bicycle. As for Paul Drake, he is taken by various buses to Burbank, Torrance and Santa Monica, and ends with no hope of immediate return, at Redondo Beach. He only hears about Diana's suicide on the radio. Days afterward, Perry

Mason is able to close the file with the words, "And so ends the Case of the Automotiveless Detective." Without a car the Defense Attorney is so hampered that the next tragedy overtakes the investigation of the last, the District Attorney winning the case before the defending counsel has even appeared. So far from ending up in triumph, the case, in this instance, could never so much as begin.

The car is not so much a vehicle as a way of life. It creates, to begin with, the modern suburbs and exurbs in which most people live. Commuters are mostly of two kinds: those who drive from home to office and those who drive to the commuter station and so reach the city by rail. To either process the automobile is essential. It is true that this pattern of life was first evolved in an age of steam locomotives and horsed carriages, but the car has brought to millions the way of life once reserved for the few. And among these millions status depends, broadly speaking, on the distance between home and office. The more remote residential areas have a more rural setting, and their exurbanite residents are senior enough to arrive late at the office. Men will thus travel daily anything from ten to sixty miles, returning over the same distance when the day's brief toil is over. This pattern of life has its effect upon the cost of administration, upon the size of the newspaper, upon the radio programs and roadside advertisements. More to our present purpose, it transfers social life from the city to the suburb, with results which are often ignored. Perhaps least noticed of any result is the breakdown of the system by which people used to live among neighbors whose business was more or less the same as theirs.

If we look at the older cities of the world, we find that they had (and sometimes still have) quarters, streets and coffee houses reserved by tradition for underwriters, medical men, tailors or artists. Paris has thus its Latin Quarter, London its Harley Street, Fleet Street, Savile Row or Chelsea, New York its Wall Street and Greenwich Village. These were or are areas where like-minded people lived or live, frequenting the same places of entertainment. Excellence was the result of cooperation and rivalry between mathematicians, painters, actors, musicians, scholars, criminals, booksellers and lawyers. And people originally lived where they worked, attended the same churches and concert halls and argued fiercely round the tables of the same taverns or cafés. Theirs was in fact the life of the city. Contrast with this the pattern produced by the commuter train. At nightfall the lawyers, engineers, professors and opera singers disperse in all directions, traveling a distance which is proportioned to their family circumstances and income. In the suburb of his choice, the architect finds that his immediate neighbors include a public accountant, a bookmaker, an assistant bank manager and a civil servant. Architects of his own type are scattered round the city in different directions and varying distances, but there is none he can meet in the evening without a complex peripheral drive. With his neighbors he can talk gardening or play bridge, but intellectual stimulus in his own field of interest must be derived more from his professional journal than from personal contact. Suburban differs from city life mainly in thus isolating people of specialized knowledge.

If there is a sense in which the car has killed the city, there is also a sense in which it is killing the countryside. The life of the village droops as folk are drawn thence to the market town. The market town becomes a dormitory of the nearest city or else a city in its own right. Suburbs extend over areas which used to be agricultural, linking industrial centers which were formerly distinct. The resulting conurbation is a sprawling series of similar suburbs, characterless, shapeless and apparently endless.

From the point of view of material comfort the suburb has much to commend it. Suburbs are relatively quiet, clean and safe, with gardens for the children and schools within easy reach. They are free, moreover, from the municipal corruption which has done so much to make the big city uninhabitable. When all this is admitted, the fact remains that they represent a compromise between the urban and the rural life, largely missing the point of either. So far, and for this reason, the suburb has never attracted the sort of loyalty which once centered upon the city or village. Residents are too transient, for one thing, and their allegiance is divided. Working in London, Chicago or Boston, they make their homes in Surrey, Indiana or New Hampshire. If they are loyal to anything smaller than their country, it is to the make of car they usually purchase. For it is on the automobile that their whole way of life depends. If they can take it with them to the city, they will, regardless of parking problems and traffic jams. It is the craze for speed which brings everything to a standstill.

Automotionless traffic is thus a feature of city life, reaching its daily crisis when everyone heads for the suburb at the same time. Having formed the suburb and wrecked the city, the car has gone on to create the long weekend and the short vacation, the cabin cruiser and the ski resort. All of these diversions depend upon automobility. Without the car they would never have begun and without the car they could never survive.

With the automobile came the need for the garage as a

feature of the home. The previous need, where carriage folk were concerned, was for a coach house, harness room and stables, all placed well away from the house. Horses attract flies, so that this separation was justified. Nor was it otherwise inconvenient, for the carriage or the horse for riding would be brought round to the front door at the proper hour as timed by the stable yard clock. The horseless carriage took its place in the coach house, inheriting the accepted ideas about distance; rationalized, sometimes, by talk of fire risk. Architecturally, the garage was an afterthought, as it often still remains — a place to be reached by a twenty-yard sprint in the pouring rain.

The architects who borrowed this aspect of nineteenth-century design were apt to overlook another feature, which might have been more obviously useful — the porte-cochere, or car port, as it is now called. Having done what we can to protect our own vehicle from the elements, we are not wildly quixotic if we decide to protect our guest's vehicle as well. Of the twentieth-century home we might fairly expect that the lady visitor's frock should not be exposed to the snow nor her car parked, of necessity, in the glare of the sun. If that were our expectation, however, we should soon be undeceived. No such logic has influenced us, and each new house has been no more than a modification of what has gone before, planned to advertise the architect's cleverness or flatter the client's consequence.

At any home of above a certain size, the recurrence of the cocktail party can, surely, be assumed. If we suppose that there is room for sixty, that will be the number for which we have to cater. Our hospitality must extend, therefore, to perhaps forty automobiles. How are they to enter or leave, and where are they to park? There are homes where the traffic problem has been closely studied, fully discussed and triumphantly solved. Far more numerous, however, are the homes where it has been blandly ignored, halfheartedly considered or left finally to chance. These provide the background to those frenzied appeals which interrupt the party at its height: "Would the owner of the Ford, 72384 . . ." Or else the agitated host is seen going from group to group, asking about the gray Lincoln. "That would be Brenda's — no, I remember, though, she brought a compact. Tell me, someone, whose is the Ford? Lewis has to leave early but is boxed in . . . Ah, Sam — could that be your Ford in the driveway? No? It must belong to *somebody* . . ." All this fuss and bother stems from the original mistake in planning.

So far as the suburban world is concerned, the car is here for keeps. Learning how to live with it, we must enable it also to live with us. Its behavior is better when it is treated with consideration, and it is naturally offended when its needs are overlooked. Of the home of the future the automobile must be an integral part, its garage no afterthought but a planned and covered space for the car's essential rest and recreation.

In his classic work *The Exurbanites,* Spectorsky describes the technique of driving a jeep to the commuter station in such a way as to indicate that the Cadillac is taking the children to school. He thus draws our attention to the multi-automotive family. The second car for the wife is but a step toward the third car for the children, thus bringing us to what has been called the Teen-age Problem. This is created less by adolescent psychology than by this phenomenon of multi-automotivity. The parents' reluctant purchase of car No. 3 is the result of a desire to retain the use of cars Nos. 1

and 2. The purchase completed, the teen-agers begin to live a life of their own.

The problem which this creates is not one of psychology but of transport. To understand this, we have to draw a comparison with the society in which our grandparents lived. Their world was ruled, above all, by middle-class morality. Under Queen Victoria and President Lincoln, there was a long and lengthening list of things forbidden, more especially on the Sabbath. The Lord's Day assumed a rigid pattern in which family prayers and divine service alternated with staid perambulation and ritual civility. Top hats were raised in stately greeting and church bells summoned the faithful to prayer. A heavy midday meal foreshadowed a somnolent afternoon and justified that cold supper which would enable the servants to attend evensong. Evening fell upon towns and villages which were apparently lifeless, with but rare footsteps echoing from the pavement of deserted streets. Unseen by the stranger were the curtained and gaslit interiors. Everything, but *everything,* was closed.

Chief sufferers from Sabbatarianism were the children. For the boys there was the stiff collar and Sunday-best suit, for the girls a dress of rustling and starched discomfort. Came the bustle of preparing for church, with the distribution of prayer books and collection money. Sermons were long and theological, pews were hard and floors were cold. Nor did religious observance stop at that, for the Sabbath day school claimed the afternoon for its own, interposing between one service and the next. Outdoor games were forbidden and Sunday clothes made them, anyway, all but impracticable. Indoors, the Noah's Ark might be the only plaything allowed, and reading matter had to be of the most Improving kind. There is something irritating about arbitrary rules of obscure origin, but their literal observance can be easier than was at first intended. For the ban on organized games was never extended, as it should logically have been, to the pastimes of which the Victorian Deity had never heard; to the flying, for example, of model aircraft. Neither was cycling forbidden in a community to which the horse and buggy had been important, and necessary even for going to church.

It was the bicycle, in fact, which loosened the whole fabric of the Victorian Sabbath. For the bicycle took its rider into another parish or county, far from his neighbors' and parents' disapproving eyes. He might have gone there to attend a different church. He might equally have gone to catch butterflies or paint landscapes in watercolor. He might still encounter hostile glances from behind lace curtains, but they came from people who did not know who he was or whence he came. In bringing the freedom of anonymity, the cycle left the old morality dead. All the car did was to take the truant still further afield, leaving him free to sunbathe, swim or flirt. Even more than the bicycle, it extended the same freedom to women. Whatever they chose to do, they could do it somewhere else.

The Teen-age Problem is thus inseparable from the automobile. If young people plunge into discreditable activities, it is not because they live in Peyton Place but because they have the means of escaping from it. Worried parents counter this with the family weekend, taking the children with them to the nearest lake or seaside resort. This is effective only in so far as the parents are willing to engage in teen-age activities. Even this sacrifice only postpones for a while the automotional problems which are bound to arise. For, granted that parents are glad to go sailing with their children, the time will soon come when the children would rather go sailing by themselves. It is the third car which makes this possible, creating all the complications which go to make the modern novel so tedious. To the whole subject of teenology we shall have to return, but some brief mention of it was inevitable in any discussion of automobility.

As a method of moving from place to place, pedestrianism is now so unfashionable as to be thought (at best) eccentric. To walk on the golf course is allowable, at the airport inevitable, but elsewhere it is almost unknown. There are instances, to be sure, of cars being parked further from their destination than they were at their point of departure. Such rare occasions apart, however, the custom is to drive rather than walk and the body has to adjust itself to inactivity.

The Automobilious Syndrome is well illustrated in the advertising pages of the American magazine. First advertisements to catch the eye are those which glamorize the automobile. Shining, immaculate, deep-cushioned and luxurious, the most expensive cars are shown standing outside the most exclusive buildings. We fall for this glimpse of gracious living and turn to the next page. This depicts food in the realistic way which only Americans ever attempt. Virginia ham glows in Technicolor from amid slices of pineapple. Steak sizzles along with mushrooms, and cream billows over the chocolate cake. We fall for this in turn, agreeing that only the best is good enough. This idea is confirmed again by the picture overleaf of some fabulous brandy in balloon glasses, posed among the Georgian silver and reflected in the polished mahogany. It all suggests the mood in which a perfect dinner should end.

Sighing happily, we turn to the next advertisement, one published by a famous shipping line. From this we learn that a world cruise can be so arranged that Naples, Athens and Istanbul are brought to you for your inspection. With out leaving your deck chair, except at mealtimes, you can see all that is worth seeing of antiquity or scenic interest. Should you go ashore, nevertheless, a Cadillac will await your pleasure, bringing you back to the ship in time for the evening's entertainment. Once more impressed, we turn the page again.

But here the shock awaits us, for the next pictures are of beautiful and expensive clothes. In sophisticated surroundings the most elegant people are all superbly dressed. To wear those dresses, however, to wear those suits, they are all streamlined to the point of starvation, slim beyond hope of imitation. No one who had relaxed in that car, eaten that dinner, drunk that brandy and completed that cruise could possibly get into those clothes. The whole trend of the sequence is to ask the impossible. Shocked and saddened, we hasten to see how the story ends. Overleaf once more we find an advertisement for a slimming treatment, "How to overeat without being overweight." It is obvious nonsense, but we mop our foreheads with relief. Help is at hand! We can have our cake and eat it. We can be greedy, inactive *and* slim!

Happy in this thought, we pass on to the last advertisement, just before the magazine's table of contents. "Are you being killed by worry?" asks the headline. Well, come to think of it, that is exactly what is happening. Slimming drugs may be very well but what of their side effects? Are we not running an appalling risk? Shall we not end as drug addicts? No, for this last advertisement tells us of the tranquilizer which alone can save us, banishing our anxiety and allowing us to relax. We turn back to the glittering automobile, reflecting that our own is now two years old. It is time to trade it in and acquire something which will add to our status. Shall it be the saloon or the more dashing convertible?

Still more to the point, we have come to accept the car as a means of expression, an extension of our personality. To the housewife, Car No. 2 is far more than a means of reaching the school or supermarket, just as a hat is far more than a mere protection of the head. She chooses the car as she chooses her clothes and with the same attention to fashion, style, color and shape. The car is a garment, worn outside the muskrat or mink and conveying its own subtle message of self-assurance, caution or defiance. Car No. 1 in the family is the husband's mistress, her opulence the proof of his infatuation. Car No. 2 is male, the wife's current gigolo. The infidelity is, in this instance, more discreet, the decencies observed. In the very early years of the marriage, Car No. 2 may be an old friend or rejected suitor, a relic of student days. The car which supplants the old flame represents a more definite gesture. It expresses not only the personality but the mood. Thus, where the store has attempted to overcharge, the car drives off with a snort of contempt. When it overtakes the car of a social rival, it does so with elaborate unconcern, seemingly unaware of the other car's presence. When halted for speeding, its wide-eyed innocence echoes that of its driver. "What, *me??*" it seems to say, the tone suggesting that it was stationary at the time, if not actually moving slowly in reverse.

The automobile is, finally, a subject of conversation, of a sort that has its origin, of course, in our ancestors' twaddle about horses and carriages. One of the earliest highway bores in literature is the Dauphin in Shakespeare's *Henry V* (Act III, Scene VII):

Dauphin:	It is a beast for Perseus: he is pure air and fire; and the dull elements of earth and water never appear in him, but only in patient stillness while his rider mounts him: he is, indeed, a horse; and all other jades you may call beasts.
Constable:	(*Bored to tears*) Indeed, my Lord, it is a most absolute and excellent horse.
Dauphin:	It is the prince of palfreys; his neigh is like the bidding of a monarch, and his countenance enforces homage.
Orleans:	(*Desperate*) No more, cousin.
Dauphin:	. . . I once writ a sonnet in his praise, and began thus: "Wonder of nature," . . .

Shakespeare spares us the sonnet, which came later to be paraphrased in honor of the horsed carriage. Knowing all about it, Jane Austen created the imbecile John Thorpe, a minor but essential character in *Northanger Abbey.*

"What do you think of my gig, Miss Morland?" is his opening and he asks her to guess what the vehicle cost. "Curricle-hung, you see; seat, trunk, sword-case, splashing-board, lamps, silver moulding, all, you see, complete; the ironwork as good as new, or better. . . ."

Revealing presently that it cost him fifty guineas, he evidently expects her to make some suitable exclamation. This Catherine fails to do, having no idea whether it was cheap or dear. "Neither one nor t'other," he explains, adding (a) that he might have got it for less but hated to be mean and that (b) he might have sold it next day for ten guineas more. He is the classic prototype of the automobore.

Even the most ordinary car can thus be made an instrument of conversational torture. Agony can be inflicted in talk about how to reach the Kingston bypass without encountering the traffic lights in Muddlecombe. Then there is the character who owns either a veteran or a foreign car, with a prestigious name like Isotto-Fraschini; a Lamborghini 350 GT2 + 2 coupé, maybe, altered in some way so as to resemble no other, or else perhaps a Miura of the very first vintage. The Dauphin's babbling about his horse foreshadows more contemporary chatter about horespower:

Dauphin: . . . I will not change my horse with any that treads but on four pasterns. . . . When I bestride him, I soar, I am a hawk: he trots the air; the earth sings when he touches it; the basest horn of his hoof is more musical than the pipe of Hermes.

How readily this becomes: "I would not change my car for any on four wheels. When I drive it I soar, I am a hawk: it flies through space; the roadway sings beneath it and there is music in its horn!"

Last of all comes the pundit whose conversation is not about the car but about its entrails, its virility and its ailments.

"The Panther Barracada III is a magnificent car, as I'm the first to admit. With its 4-litre V-12 engine, its six gears and 10,000 rpm, it can do 165 mph with ease. Its acceleration is all anyone could ask. But why did they spoil the job with that stupid positioning of the cam sprocket? Surely you must have noticed? You didn't? Well, it's quite simple to explain. In Model I, the prototype produced in 1965, the slotted shaft was a little inclined to shift after the first 5000 miles. They cured *that* by adding that other sleeve just forward of the locking pin. What they didn't foresee was the vibration which would result in the differential ratchet. It vibrates so much that the rivets come loose round the synchronized rotor head. They are only copper, of course, and subject to metal fatigue. Replacing them, you might just as well have a new differential and have done with it, but the engine is so placed that you cannot touch the rotor head without removing the whole distributor section. It amounts, of course, to stripping the whole engine! Then there's another thing. I daresay you remember the baseplate that you have to have with any engine mounted sideways across the chassis? Well, the Panther III has its own version of that but welded — not bolted — to the frame. What can they have been thinking of? It had been bolted, of course, in the original design but this welding was supposed to be an *improvement*. Can you imagine it? The bearings can only stand so much and the V-12 engine is no lightweight. Nothing has actually gone wrong as yet but — well, we'll see. One of these days the whole engine in one of these cars will shift! Not in mine, though. Can you guess what I have done to prevent it?"

Let us suppose that the modern John Thorpe is addressing a shy girl of eighteen who has never so much as looked under a car's hood. She has been too polite to interrupt him and she feels even now that she must attempt to show some interest.

"Perhaps you glued it down with rubber cement?"

"Aha! Very smart, Jane. No, I made them add a steel bracket on either side of the radiator, bolted to the frame. Quite simple, really. They could have done it so easily in the first place! Guess what it cost!"

One would like to end the scene by making the girl reply, "A million dollars" before laying him prostrate with a bronze statuette of the Venus de Milo. In point of fact, she would admit tamely that she had no idea.

"Fourteen dollars and fifty cents!" Like Catherine Morland, she still does not know whether this is supposed to be cheap or dear. She plays safe by exclaiming:

"Is that right? For Pete's sake!"

"I swear that's all it cost. And for that I have what is almost a different car. I'll trade it in next year, of course, and possibly buy a Puma-Porpoise. Have you seen their new model, Type F?"

She has never heard of the Puma-Porpoise and is, in any case, only longing to escape. Let us, in all humanity, end the scene by allowing her to do so. Enter, let us hope, a loud-voiced automobully, who overhears the last words.

"The Puma-Porpoise?" he exclaims. "No one in his senses would drive a P-P — not even you, George. Be your age, man! The Type F model is so badly designed that it will be on the scrap heap next year. Listen to this, Bill — here's George landing himself with — of all things — a P-P Type F!" While the other men cluster around, Jane makes her exit. Shuddering, she thinks what it would be like to have married an automobully. That, she rightly concludes, is the fate that is *really* worse than death.

CHAPTER FOUR

Home on the Range

TWO MAIN FACTORS govern the design, construction and equipment of the home. First of these is that no one man or woman can be held responsible for its success or failure. A surgeon (by contrast) removes an appendix, an artist paints a picture and a lawyer wins or loses his case, each being answerable for the result. But a house is the joint work of owners, architects, planners, electricians and decorators. No one man can sign the finished canvas. The work has been done, rather, by a motley team, some members of which are barely on speaking terms with the owners or each other, while many are seemingly unaware that the others exist. The result is the home in which we have to live and the range upon which some of us will have to cook.

It might seem, at the outset, that the division of responsibility may be the cause, at least in part, of the appallingly slow progress that has been observable in domestic architecture. It is the unfortunate fact, moreover, that improvements in design have been largely negatived by our declining standards of workmanship. There was a brief and blissful period in history (1890-1910) when twentieth-century plans were carried out by nineteenth-century workmen. Such vintage homes are scarce, however, and the choice for most of us is between what is well-constructed but badly planned and what is of contemporary design but badly built.

The second factor is that men have been planning, for women, equipment which they, the men, will not have to use. Such recent progress as there has been is almost solely due to men being compelled, almost for the first time, to use the machinery they have designed for the home. Men were concerned with the garden before they ever entered the kitchen, the result being the lawn mower and, more recently, the power mower or autoscythe. The immediate result of asking their help with the dirty crockery was the dishwasher. Women have lacked the imagination to design these things for themselves. Lazy, and for that reason more inventive, men have used the machine to forestall the demand for help.

Women have simultaneously become more assertive of their rights, making men the less inclined to assist them. Home mechanization would have been more rapid, perhaps, had women been less independent in their attitude. By being more helpless, they could hardly have fared worse. In the situation that exists, women have been consoled with electrical equipment for their lack of domestic help. The electric motors in a comfortable home may number up to thirty, and the logical answer would be to build the house around its equipment. In practice the building comes first and the machinery is crammed in afterward, the vacuum cleaner in the shoe cupboard, the air conditioner hanging out of a first-floor window and the television aerial bolted to an otherwise useless chimney.

Bearing these two factors in mind, let us now explore the average middle-class home, beginning at the front door and ending in the attic. When we open the front door in winter, an arctic gale sweeps through the house, there being no in-

Osborn

ner door to prevent it, and so we find ourselves in the entrance hall, where no provision has been made for our overcoats. Hooks there may be on the wall but there is often no alternative to some protruding piece of furniture: a hatstand, a wardrobe or a settee. This makes narrower what was already narrow enough and we note, at the outset, that there is no space here for the perambulator. It exists, has existed for years, and the need for it will recur, but no architect or builder has ever heard of it. It either blocks the passage to the kitchen or is wheeled into the garage where it prevents the car door from opening. The car door on the *other* side is similarly blocked by the children's bicycles. Only an imbecile, it is true, would have designed a car door to open outward. Such imbeciles exist, however, and so do the bicycles and tricycles which cumber our path. Observe in passing that the house's number or name is carefully hidden — especially at night — and that the letter box or slot is too small for the periodicals which may be expected. There may or may not be a sunken place for the doormat — over which we will otherwise trip — and there may or may not be an external light.

To left or right is the living room, where the central feature is a tiled fireplace of probably hideous appearance, the architectural setting for a gas or electric fire. We realize at once that this is a symbol of a past way of life. Focal point of indoor activity in winter was the chimneypiece, the glowing logs or peat, the center for warmth and light and conversation. Grandparents might sit in the chimney corners, parents on either side of the hearth, children and dogs in the center and distant cousins removed (and if necessary *twice* removed) to some suitable distance. When about to exert his authority or display his wisdom, father had to stand on the hearthrug with his back to the fire and his hands beneath his coattails. Only when so placed could he disinherit his wastrel son or forbid his erring daughter to cross the threshold. The older tradition of family life involved a visible center, with authority and seniority well defined and with everyone (literally) knowing his place.

This for long remained true in Britain and the United States, where coal was cheap, but less so on the European continent where people tended to rely more upon enclosed stoves. Each year the British still vainly offer for sale in Europe those electric fires in which a flickering red glow counterfeits the effect of logs or coal; articles readily sold in England but meaningless in countries where the open fire has been unknown since the Middle Ages. What has largely killed the open fire in the U.S.A. and Britain is not a passion for central heating but the lack of domestic servants. So long as there were people available to carry laden buckets from the bin or logs from the woodshed to the fireside, there were other people ready to pay them to do it. But the carrying of coal or wood up three flights of stairs must become burdensome when no longer done by deputy. Our heating tends now to be central and the fireplace which remains has lost its point. It is often still there, however, a vestigial relic of a past way of life.

The modern living room is no longer the space around the hearth. It has become a miniature theater, based upon the television set. Chairs are grouped as in a cinema, thrust aside only when guests appear, and a general lighting has been replaced by standard lamps for the odd eccentric who may want to read. But the sad facts of life are not reflected in the architecture. There is seldom an alcove into which the flickering screen can be built. The television set, like the radio, remains an excrescence, an intrusion upon a family life still theoretically centered upon the hearth. No living room is planned with the television set, or alternative screen, in open possession of what would once have been the fireplace.

Realizing this, we look around to see what other features reflect, or fail to reflect, the life we actually live. We thus notice the absence of a picture molding, a Victorian fitting which assumed, and rightly, that wall decorations are likely to be hung. This assumption is still correct, but the sheet rock or plaster has now to be drilled and plugged, damaging the surface and offering the interesting possibility that the drill will make contact with an electric cable hidden in the plasterwork. No builder ever obviates this inconvenience by inserting a wooden rail, flush with the surface, at a standard distance from the ceiling. In rather the same way the window pelmets are no part of the room's design but an inevitable afterthought, an occasion for more hammering and drilling, intrusion and mess. While the architect has failed to foresee the need for curtains, the electrician *has* anticipated the need for standard lamps, vacuum cleaners and television, spoiling the effect by placing his wildly unstandardized plugs at floor level where they are most likely to be damaged. Defects such as these are repeated throughout the house but will not be the subject of further comment.

The dining room or "dining area" is adjacent to the kitchen, with which it is often connected by a serving hatch; a useful device on the Edwardian assumption that you have domestic servants on the other side of it. Where the housewife has to cope unaided, her need is really for a connecting door, for want of which she has to go round via the entrance hall. This implies the use of a serving cart, the propulsion of which leaves one hand free to open and close the intervening doors. Serving its primary purpose well, the cart has nowhere to go when not in use. It will stand somewhere in the kitchen, blocking a cupboard doorway or so placed that everyone falls over it. Where there *is* a door rather than a hatch, it will have to be pushed open by the tray-carrier's bottom and there will be no way of screening the kitchen from the guests at table.

Essential to the dining room is the storage space for table mats, tablecloth, napkins, sherry, corkscrew, ashtrays, candles and plate. No such space is provided, and a cumbersome sideboard meets a need which the architect should have foreseen. It spoils the proportions, such as they are, of the room and reduces the space available for circulation round the table. It is the total floor space, minus the sideboard, which suggests the size and shape of the table. This can be either oblong, circular or oval (never square), and the chairs may number from six to twelve. In the ideal, as opposed to the typical, dining room, the plan should have been drawn with some definite number in mind.

We come now to the heart of the matter: home on the range. The kitchen is the housewife's workshop, the place where she has most scope for imagination and economy, for science and art. This is the battlefield upon which she must triumph or admit defeat. Let us suppose that our visit coincides with her return, laden, from the supermarket. As soon as she enters by the back door one defect in the kitchen plan is instantly apparent. For a feature of our age is the superabundance of its wrapping paper. In the name of hygiene and paper-manufacturing dividends, everything from the bread (which is dietetically worthless) to the eggs (laid weeks ago by battery-fed prisoners) must be protected by cardboard or paper, by cellophane or foil. The daily accumulation is almost frightening in its mere bulk. But no one seems to have any plan for its disposal. Stuffing the paper into a sack hung behind the door, putting her purchases in the refrigerator or cupboard, the housewife turns to an object which is central to her life: the Sink. . . . Fifty years ago the sink was an oblong, shallow trough of yellowish earthenware, placed far enough under a tap to allow for a bucket being filled there. Its sides were grooved like those white plates which are now only exported to Canada, and it was fitted with a drainpipe and plug. When the time came to wash the dishes, the first move was to boil a kettle and the second move was to pour hot water, diluted with cold, into a chipped enamel basin which was placed in the sink. Since those early days, the March of Progress has introduced a second tap, which actually runs hot, and has altered the appearance and shape of the sink itself. It first became whiter and deeper, then it turned into stainless steel, the grooved wooden draining boards being transformed into shining metal or gaily colored Formica, the old wooden plate racks turning into fiber glass or plastic.

What is surprising, however, is that the old basin (now also made in plastic) should remain; a smaller basin *within* a larger trough. But *why?* Why should not the sink be of the right size to begin with? Perhaps a hundred years of mental effort have at last produced a double sink, each half small enough to fill directly as a first step toward washing the dishes. But houses with double sinks are still the exception and those with plastic basins are still the rule. Nor is even the double sink complete, for the housewife needs to add, as she has always done, a triangular perforated vessel into which her wet trash and tea leaves can be emptied. Without this the drainpipe is likely to be blocked, as the designer of the sink should have realized. But why was no effort made to produce a sink that was complete in itself, needing no plastic afterthought? Why was not the required mesh incorporated in the original design? It is true that the waste-disposal unit is now on the market, but how long it has taken to appear! Seldom, in the story of human domesticity, has so little thought been devoted to a piece of equipment used by so many for so much of their time.

Turning from the sink and looking about us, we realize that the Victorian kitchen, with its scullery, pantry and larder, its range and its boiler, its boot cupboards and coal bin, was at least designed for its purpose. In this modern kitchen, by contrast, the stove and water heater, the refrigerator and dishwasher are all so many optional extras, each crammed somehow into a room for which there is no planned layout. The need for everything might have been foreseen, but the shape and size of each unit was impossible to anticipate and might easily change. So far from being designed, the kitchen is haphazardly thrown together and chronically untidy. Cupboard units have been installed but with a total capacity inferior to that of the pantry our parents had. The refrigerator is essential but its cubic content is a mere fraction of what the larder would have contained had there been one.

The kitchen, let's face it, is a mess; and using one end as breakfast room will often make it worse. Where there is a third reception room, sometimes called the breakfast room and sometimes called the study, it is either the warmest or the coldest place in the house and is often disused save as an occasional refuge from television.

Beneath the American ground floor there is often a basement which contains, besides the heating plant, a workshop and rumpus room; the playing areas for men, respectively, and children. British homes are often without either, tools and toys invading the rest of the house. Where rumpus rooms are concerned, the U.S.A. still leads the world.

Central problem of the ground-floor rooms is that of tidiness. It is obvious that all the efforts at decoration, all the care spent on choosing wallpaper and curtaining material, are wasted on the untidy home, for the disorder will be all that the visitor sees. The more impoverished Victorians overcame this problem by setting aside a parlor which they never entered except on the rare occasions when the Vicar called. Such a parlor was always in perfect order by the standards of the day, but its chilly existence deprived them of the space they needed, reducing the effective size of a house already quite small enough. This is a mistake we have learned to avoid, but the penalty has been to spread the kitchen's disorder into the rooms adjacent. The same space has to be used for working and chattering, for entertaining and correspondence, for homework and hobbies, for music and chess. The result is that process by which the litter from the last activity is still around when the current occupation is giving place to the next. It is in surroundings of chronic disorder that many people choose to live, their time largely wasted in hunting for scissors or cookbook, for pencils or string. In their home, as in the midshipman's sea chest, there is everything on top and nothing to be found.

A great textbook on tidiness remains to be written, with chapters on theory and practice, with footnotes, bibliography, appendices and index. It would be shown, from historical example, that tidiness is easier where space is sufficient, with attics and cupboards, with outbuildings and cellars. It would be proved from case histories and depth interviews that the best workmen cannot even begin work before they have brushed the floor and laid out their tools in their accustomed sequence. It could be argued, on the other hand, that the most precise order has its origin in the more confined space. Where men live under canvas or at sea they are often compelled by their surroundings to keep everything, literally, shipshape. Whatever may be needed, from a rope to a rifle, can be found in pitch darkness within a matter of seconds. Tidiness can thus be made to seem an aspect of efficiency.

But is it? For some work is always performed under conditions of squalor. Backstage at the theater is always chaos and so are the working parts of a television studio. What is true, moreover, of an English cabinetmaker or research scientist is quite untrue of the Chinese woodcarver or joiner. The most intricate patterns are carved by Chinese workmen on the sidewalks of busy streets amid a confusion of hawkers and children and poultry and dogs. Nor is the tidiness of a British warship repeated faithfully on the deck of a Cantonese junk, which nevertheless earns its living and makes its landfall. The truth is that tidiness is not so much practically necessary as it is aesthetically and psychologically satisfying.

Tidiness means keeping things out of sight and yet available when wanted. It implies that there is a place for everything and that each thing used finds its way back to its place by a continuous process, not by a spasmodic effort. The process depends, however, upon the drawer, cupboard and storage space being provided, for lack of which some things may literally have no place to go. Like the perambulator and cart, the luggage and the golf clubs may be homeless. The same may be true of the deck chairs and the bulkier plastic toys. As there is no place for them, it is no good telling people to put them away. The architect who thus economizes on storage space is apt to claim that a good-sized living room is the result. What advantage is there in that, however, when half the living room has to be used for storage?

The aesthetic appeal of a home depends upon order as well as beauty; and order depends, in turn, upon storage space. While it may be true that no house ever had cupboards enough, there are some houses which have practically no cupboards at all. In these our choice must lie between chronic untidiness and ruthless destruction. That is not to say, however, that cupboard space will itself create tidiness. Some people are happier, it would seem, in chaos. There is the question, furthermore, whether the cupboards themselves are tidy. That everything has been swept out of sight is no proof, in itself, that anything can be found.

It is time now to go upstairs, should this be possible. In point of fact, the modern house is often on one floor; a natural response, it would seem, to our shortage of ground suitable for development. What the psychological result may be on the children is a matter, at present, for surmise. It may be true that a childhood spent in a house without a staircase will produce an adult without ambition. It may also be true that a deprivation of banisters to slide down will rob the young of courage. Certain it is that a triumphant ascent of the staircase is, for many infants, the first great achievement. It is for this reason, no doubt, that the house on two floors is still the rule rather than the exception.

And central to the upper floor, in Britain, is a single bathroom and (possibly) a separate toilet. There are countries in which every bedroom has a bathroom attached, but Britain is not one of them. Living in the dirtiest country in the world, we are content to wait our turn for the bath. And when our turn finally comes we find that the bath is an extraordinary product, apparently changeless in shape and arbitrary in design. Baths in the U.S.A. are more numerous than in Britain but what they gain in frequency they lose in size. Some puritanical tradition underlies the American bath in which one can sit but cannot lie. Cleanliness is not to be made the excuse for luxury. From the first century of progress, moreover, the man who made the British or American bath remained ignorant of the existence of soap. The bath, he felt, was enough in itself; we could not possibly want soap *as well*. In point of fact we *did* and the result was a variety of soap dishes and sponge racks added to the bath with varying degrees of ingenuity and success. The thing as manufactured has never been complete and ready for use. It has taken literally generations of effort to produce a bath in which the need for soap is actually assumed.

As for the shower, its problems have not been solved yet. The taps are usually so placed that the water temperature can be adjusted only by someone who is already in the shower, the guinea pig of his own experiment. With water nearly boiling there may be no means, in fact, of turning the thing off. It is true that Americans have devised a glass screen which at least obviates the flooding of the bathroom. But the mirror-fronted cupboard in which we keep bath salts and shaving cream is often still an excrescence screwed to the wall. The need for it could be foreseen but seldom had anyone thought to build it into the wall.

This is a logical point at which to pause and consider the subject of electrical fittings. In the U.S.A., more particularly, we hear much of rugged individualism but see much more of tame conformity. Rugged individuals exist, however, both there and in Britain, and most of them are obviously electricians. Modern oil paintings and hit tunes may be identical, but each electric fitting is a separate work of art. Let us suppose, to illustrate this point, that a European guest is about to retire for the night in an hospitable American home. Saying good night to his host, who is taking the dog for a walk, the guest finds his room without difficulty, humming, it may be, a gay snatch of song. As the room is unlighted he feels for the switch, assuming that it will be just inside the door, at shoulder height and on the side opposite the hinge. There is none to be found either by feel or by the light from the corridor.

He sidles further into the room and, as he does so, the door closes itself, leaving him in pitch darkness. In panic he abandons the search for the switch and seeks only to rediscover the door. This time he manages to leave it slightly open as he begins to reconnoiter in the opposite direction. There is no switch there either, but a sudden collision with a presumably T'ang vase leaves him clutching the porcelain while being tickled under the chin by its all too silken fringe. The thing is a lampstand and should be controlled by a switch just beneath the bulb, but there is nothing there to manipulate. The search continues with crash and bump, ending for the moment when the traveler falls over the foot of the bed. It occurs to him that there should be a reading light over the pillow. So there is, but without a switch. . . .

The guest decides to begin again but this time in the adjacent bathroom, admittedly darker but presumably less encumbered with furniture. Assuming that the bathroom mirror should be capable of illumination, patience should triumph in the end. A methodical search now reveals that the bathroom has everything that one might expect and some refinements upon which one would not have dared to count, but lacks only an electric light switch. Sitting on the edge of the bath, the guest feels an interesting series of handles and levers. One, differing in shape from the rest, might possibly be the switch. Touching it gingerly brings on an instant downpour of tropical intensity. Removing his soaked jacket and drying his hair, the alarmed guest rings what he takes to be the bell. The room is instantly lit by the fluorescent light over the mirror.

With courage renewed and light streaming from the bathroom, the guest turns back to the bedroom with a song (more or less) in his heart. Nor is he disappointed. Inspection of the half-lit room now reveals something hitherto unnoticed, a flexible cord hanging from the ceiling over the middle of the bed. It is also now apparent that the standard lamps are placed opposite two outlets in the baseboard, and merely need to be plugged in. One lights up as soon as connected, the other only when he has rotated the shade. A further plug serves a hitherto unnoticed radio, which promptly obliges with music. A switch beneath the dressing table starts the air conditioner, and life is now a different thing.

There remains, however, the cord and knob dangling over the bedspread and the guest decides to discover what it is for. A light pressure on the button produces a faint click and all the lights are extinguished, even in the bathroom. A second hurried pressure produces no result at all. The only thing unaffected is the radio, from which a woman's voice is audible, tense with sympathy. "Do you lose your temper when things go wrong? Yes? You do? Then you are liverish. What you need is a spoonful of Muttsdope, to be had from any drugstore . . ." It may be the stuff for the liver (thinks the guest), but what are we to do with the lights?

It is the sad fact that electrical fittings are wildly individualistic in voltage, in plug fitting and, above all, in methods of control. Switches press upward, downward, sideways, inward and outward, each manufacturer seeking to find novelty in the area where we most need to find standardization. As with car doors, the best type of locking device is a matter of relative indifference, provided only that all are the same. But the quest for originality leaves us with a final sense of the futile. There is room, heaven knows, for progress, but not for constant variation in things which are only marginally important. Worst offender in this jungle of innovation is the electrician. With his hatred of uniformity he leaves us to struggle with the perennially unfamiliar.

What is only mildly annoying when we have time and patience becomes intolerable when we are under pressure. There may be circumstances in which we can pause and admire the ingenuity of the workmanship but there are more numerous occasions when what we want is *light.* Our faint hope is that the electrician of the future will rely less on the inspiration of the moment and more upon some conventions accepted by the trade. The exact position of an electric light switch matters far less than our foreknowledge of where it is going to be. There are fields of activity and even of interior decoration in which fantasy is acceptable, but electrical engineering is not one of them. Let us keep the light fantastic to the dance floor and content ourselves with lights which work.

It may be objected, at this point, that the defects described are a matter of cost. To obviate each one would be possible but expensive, more time being spent in planning, design and joinery. This fairly brings us back to first principles, for the present cost, already excessive, is due to the two factors described at the outset. No one man is responsible for the whole construction and no woman's convenience has been

Osborn

sufficiently analyzed. We are still building a house and cramming the equipment into it. We are not arranging the machinery and draping the house around it. If we did that, the whole process would be the work of a single engineer. So far as domestic dwellings are concerned we should scrap the architect, the builder, the electrician and the plumber. People like plasterers and bricklayers are an anachronism which we can no longer afford. A dwelling should be a factory-made unit, mass-produced like a trailer or mobile home. It should be possible to move it from one site to another, add to it or reduce it in size, replace any damaged part in a matter of minutes and erect the whole thing in a matter of hours. There is no difficulty at all in manufacturing such a dwelling and the result would be better and cheaper than anything that is now available. The plan, remember, could be a work of genius, based on years of research and study. More thought could have gone into it than into any building that was ever planned before.

There are some people who would resent standardization, thinking that it would rob them of their individuality. But the houses now built have all the appearance of being mass-produced without any of the advantages of mass production. Remember, too, that the carpets and curtains could all be made to fit a known space and that there would be a continued economy in replacement and repair. The idea of standardization is not even new, being no more than the Japanese have accepted for centuries. Herein lies the solution to our problems of accommodation, and no other solution is possible. Sooner or later our housing industry must be dragged, screaming and kicking, into the twentieth century. Will this happen, though, before the century comes to an end?

Some people would argue that a chapter on the home

should be followed by another on the garden. There will be none in this instance, for a garden is something the wise man will prefer to sacrifice. He learns about gardening, in Britain at least, from programs on television, and concludes that this activity is best left to others. For the sake of those who have not learned this lesson it will be useful to suggest what the content of these programs is. Each one begins by focusing the camera on an Outdoor Man in a tweed suit lighting his pipe against a background of impeccably drilled lettuces and broccoli.

"Good evening," he says in a smug tone of voice. "You will remember that I said something last week on the subject of Weeds. You saw how I clean between the rows of plants and you saw how the seeds should be planted, with *plenty* of compost and *plenty* of fertilizer. Today I am going to show you the results, as also the results of pruning the fruit trees. You will see how wise we were to begin making compost last year. Now, I have a guest here, Mr. Herbert Buggins, last year's Chairman of the Loamshire Horticultural Society and author of the well-known book *Insect Pests*." Another Outdoor Man appears and they greet each other, presently beginning a tour of the vegetable garden, followed by the camera.

"Fine show of string beans, Frank. You must have dug deep and watered them daily during that dry spell."

"Yes, Herbert, I watered them each day for nearly three weeks and they came through pretty well."

"Did you have any trouble with your brussels sprouts, Frank?"

"No — not this year. I had some trouble last year — yes, and the year before that — but I sprayed every single leaf last autumn. I expect you did the same in your garden?"

"No, I didn't. I uprooted all the old plants and replanted with a new stock which the insects keep away from."

"Well, Herbert, I begin to wish I had done the same. Here you see we have come to my fruit trees. I rather wanted your advice about pruning. Do you think I overdid it?"

"I wouldn't say that, Frank. The way I do it is to snip off just here, and here — and, yes, I think *here*. But it is easy to spoil the tree by pruning too much."

"And what about spraying, Herbert?"

"You can't spray too often, Frank. I am extra careful to spray the bark of the tree, not merely the leaves, using a rather stronger solution than they tell you to . . . etc . . . etc . . . etc."

British television viewers are expected to watch this sort of thing for hours. The essence of the advice conveyed is that there is nothing you can do *now*. It should have been done last February, when its efficiency would admittedly have depended upon something else having been done the previous April. So the willingness to view this sort of program is a proof of enthusiasm. Viewers must indeed be attached to the soil.

For the present purpose it will be assumed that the reader is content with a stretch of grass and an odd-job man to mow it once a week in summer. If you want more than that you should turn to some other book. You might, alternatively, reconsider your whole plan of life; for the home and the family are enough for any one man to deal with. You are simply asking for trouble if you try to keep a garden as well.

CHAPTER FIVE

Hosts and Guests

WE ARE ALL FAMILIAR, whether in life or in our reading, with the modern phenomenon known as the Stately Home. Processions of footsore people are marshaled through banqueting halls and galleries while the guide intones his ritual commentary: "Over the marble fireplace is a portrait of the Seventh Earl by Raeburn. Between the windows is a statue of John the Baptist by Basta Pasta, made for the Fifth Earl in 1678. The tapestry is Flemish and represents Moses in the Bulrushes . . ." Near the entrance is the Marquis himself, selling autographed souvenir booklets at half-a-crown a copy. Noting this trade (brisk as it may be) we may even have some passing sympathy for the landowners whose homes are thus thrown open to inspection.

It is the fact, nevertheless, that the home never visited is hardly worth the trouble of maintaining save in the bare essentials of convenience. For even the most ordinary home needs to be visited just as a book needs to be read. The artist needs a public and the play never performed is not even a play. In this sense the housewife must always be a hostess if she is to exercise her art and allow it to be seen. She also knows, or will eventually come to realize, that day-to-day appearances will deteriorate if there are no periodic and special occasions for which to make a special effort. The visit of your sister-in-law (a critical woman) is responsible for the repainting of the garden furniture. The lunch party for your old headmistress finds you eager, for some reason, to present a picture of smooth competence and worldly success.

The effort which the housewife may put into her daily tasks is thus redoubled when she has guests to welcome. But the idea of hospitality is twofold, the care to impress being coupled with a determination to ensure that no care is apparent. The hostess has to suggest, indirectly, that the effort is really effortless and that no special preparations have been made. Wordlessly she makes it clear that the table is always as highly polished, that the room is always as tidy and that the orchids were thrown into the first vase that came to hand. She knows that any hint of conscious striving for effect must ruin her image, even among people who know as well as she that the effort is inseparable from the desired result.

Let us suppose, then, that your home has been furnished and furbished down to the last silver-framed (and autographed) portrait on the piano top. The time has come to entertain your friends and neighbors, to impress whom you will have to make careful plans and work for longer hours. Work can be either artistic or menial, depending upon the individual's attitude toward what she must do. In the home, the bored and mutinous hireling sees work as something that has somehow to be finished, with money as the direct return and rest as the ultimate reward, whereas the true housewife and hostess sees rather her opportunity to show what she can do.

As between the artist and the drudge, the difference lies not in the nature of the work but in the quality of the individual's response. There is hardly anything done by anyone

glisanda

for a wage which someone else would not do (at least temporarily) for a wager. There is hardly an inconvenience known to any of us which no other person would regard as an adventure. Work is different from pastime only insofar as it goes on after we are tired of it; and people will go beyond that point even when playing a game. One secret, therefore, of happiness is to do everything artistically. To set a table for lunch is as much fun or drudgery as we care to make it and the housewife, of all people, is freest to choose. Men are in this respect less fortunate, their scope for initiative being ordinarily less. There may be, there probably is, an artistic way of balancing the company's accounts, but it offers, at first sight, less scope than would setting the table. It is as a hostess that a woman at once displays and conceals her art, impressing her neighbors and dazzling her friends. Without guests her home must be slovenly and her life incomplete. To be housewife means to be hostess as well.

A Duke who flourished at the beginning of this century was said to have four hundred indoor servants and as many outdoors to care for the thirty thousand acres of territory which surrounded just one of the several houses at which he might intermittently reside. Servants were then paid on an average about a pound a month, a moderately prosperous household employing not fewer than ten. It was further said of the same Duke that his guests, assembled for the periodic house party (each with a valet or maid as the case might be), were rarely welcomed by their host in person. There was no certainty, indeed, that they would meet him at all. His own apartments were remote and only a few of his guests were actually invited there. The rest were happy to entertain each other and glimpse the Duke on the racecourse. For most of us today hospitality is something different. As between ourselves and the Duke there is, in fact, a sharp contrast, our personal cordiality being possibly greater, our domestic help quite definitely less.

From the Duke we can learn, nevertheless, a principle of the host-and-guest relationship. Except for a very short stay there should be a measure of segregation. Why? Because a hostess with little or no domestic help must otherwise find it impossible to maintain the fiction that her hospitality is effortless. She has had to reorganize her household for the guests' benefit, and her work, beyond the weekend visit, must become the merest slavery. In the circumstances of the day the first rule of hospitality is to provide a separate guest wing or cottage with its own bathroom and kitchenette. Not everyone can afford this and not everyone wants it, but to have house guests for more than a very few days is otherwise inadvisable. Friendships are more often severed than cemented by the visit that fails.

Those ill-equipped to entertain a house party can still ask their friends to dinner, and this, we shall assume, you are prepared to do. But how many are there to be? This question brings us back to the table and where people are to sit. We all know how a hostess will scribble diagrams and bite her pencil muttering, "Suppose we put Sir George *there* and his wife *here,* with me opposite and Tony at the end — but that puts Michael next to his wife — damn!" The problem of seating is very real, being based upon a tradition which goes back to the manor hall with its dais at the far end from the door. The high table, as it is still called in college life, was placed on the dais and athwart the hall. It had benches on either side, but a chair — where there was no room for a bench — at the end of the table nearer the lord's private room or solarium. There survives from this arrangement the whole English tradition of committee work with one man, literally, in the chair (the only chair) and therefore to be described as chairman. As the master of a college still does, he looked down the table between two rows of people, half facing the body of the hall, half with their backs to it. It thus remains the English tradition that the head of the table should be reserved for the master of the house. There exists, however, an alternative plan by which the chair is moved to the center and the other seats made to flank it, all facing the hall; a later usage associated with banquets and also with girls' schools where emphasis is placed on Proper Deportment. For our present purpose this other pattern can be, and is going to be, very properly ignored.

The traditional seating plan has several socially important implications. First, the length of the table was a little less than the breadth of the hall — that being originally the length of the tree trunk which could be used as tie-beam, say, thirty feet. Give (say) two feet clearance at either end and allow two feet for each person, and there will be eleven places on either side and twenty-four places in all. Whether this was or was not the normal arrangement, the numbers six and twelve evidently came into the calculation, for knives and plates are still sold in multiples of twelve and six. Second, the table was too long for a general conversation. Nor would a general conversation have been advisable, for the number present implied a gradation in seniority and rank. Half a dozen might discuss matters of state with the master or lord. Others, of dwindling importance, would exchange their own gossip, and the young men would group themselves at the foot of the table where their improper jests would be inaudible except among themselves. At such a table there is not so much one party as about four, graded from the senior to the junior and from the sedate to the frivolous. As an arrangement it gives wonderful scope for discrimination and for giving offense, as in placing below the salt the very folk who are keenest to be above it. But the whole plan depends upon a long table, three planks broad, on its extremities being out of earshot and upon (finally) the numbers twelve and six.

Contrast with this English tradition the quite opposite customs of China and Japan. In either of these extremely civilized countries, custom decrees that the table should be circular. Why? Because it was long ago pointed out (probably by Confucius) that a round table is essential if all those present are to have equal access, with chopsticks, to the one central dish. It was also observed (no doubt by Mencius) that a round table intended for more than ten honorable persons would have an excessive radius, placing the dish out of effective reach and imposing a handicap on those who might be short in the arm. For a Chinese party, therefore, the guests are numbered, preferably, in multiples of ten. The same number is essential to Japanese custom, but there the actual party numbers five, with a geisha girl to each, making ten in all. Granted that the girls do not eat, they take up almost as much room as if they did, so that five remains the convenient maximum.

In the Far East, therefore, plates, bowls and cups are sold in multiples of five. There the accepted traditions imply that the party will be at once larger and smaller than English tradition has decreed. There are fewer people at one table but more people able to take part in one conversation. There is a measure of equality among all those present, with none condemned to sit "below the salt"; as against which, those not in the top ten will not even sit at the same table.

Students of Arthurian legend will recall that a round table was an essential feature at Camelot, but this was ring-shaped with all the knights facing inward, leaving the center free for the servants and the floor show. The table now known to us as round was first seen by English visitors to China and introduced by them into eighteenth-century England along with the tea and the chinaware. This change in furniture style went with and strengthened a different pattern of behavior. Members of the household who would formerly have found a place below the salt were now relegated to a still lower place below the floor. Society was stratified in a new sense and the round table became an established alternative to the long table of tradition. Further to complicate matters the Victorians introduced a square or oblong table, cleverly combining the disadvantages of all that had gone before. No notice will be taken of these monstrosities save to point out that their timber can often be used for something else.

For the present generation of hostesses the choice lies between the long and the round, between multiples of six and multiples of five. Should the party number five, six, eight, ten or twelve? In times past, when far larger numbers were contemplated without alarm, the meal was cooked, prepared, served and removed by a numerous domestic staff. In quite different circumstances, we may know today that twelve is as many as we can supply with crockery, glasses, knives and forks. But how many, in fact, should there be? Beginning with the lesser number, we may agree that four or even five is not a party. With six the conversation may be general but the tendency is for the talk to involve two groups of three. Eight, we find, is a difficult total if the sexes are to alternate at a long table. It leaves the hostess on one side, her rightful place taken by a male guest who may or may not be asked to serve the broccoli or asparagus. Socially, eight is undesirable except, possibly, at an oval table. What about twelve at a long table? It is almost inevitable that this should divide itself, in practice, into two parties of six or even three parties of four. What remains is the right number of ten with four on each side and the host and hostess in their proper places. With ten a general conversation is just possible, even if there should be, for much of the time, two parties of five. Granted, moreover, that the plates may initially number twelve, the party of ten has the merit of allowing for breakages. Other things being equal it is the party of ten we may most probably prefer.

Shall we dress for dinner? To dress has this advantage in the servantless house, that it discourages the guests from offering to help. Their help is not wanted, as a rule, there being no time to show them where everything is kept. As against that, dressing throws a greater burden on the hostess and perhaps even on the host. After a period of frantic activity the hostess should (in theory) descend the stairs in time to greet her guests, immaculately dressed and groomed, manicured and scented. She has to give the impression that the dinner prepared itself and that she has had two hours (rather than ten minutes) in which to bathe and change. This is more than every hostess can manage and more than every guest can believe. Most of us may conclude that we should achieve more if we attempted less. Aiming at a simpler style, we admit, by inference, that we have been working up to the last minute. Relaxed as we may be when the guests arrive, we do not actually pretend to have been at leisure all day. The hostess knows, indeed, that she must disappear again, leaving the host to act as barman while she does something urgent with the soup. Casually reappearing, she announces presently that dinner is served. There was a time (1913, say) within the memory of those still living, when the menu would have read like this:

Clear vegetable soup
Cream Comtesse

Boiled Turbot   Lobster sauce
Whitebait

Veal Cutlets Provincial

Roast Beef
Cauliflowers   New Potatoes

Boiled Chicken & Ham

Plum Tart & Custard

Maraschino Jelly

Dessert   Coffee

It is interesting to reflect that human habits change as much as they do. While people used to walk, ride or cycle, they were capable of eating that sort of dinner. In the motoring age we have lost the capacity for it. After a prawn cocktail, a cutlet and dessert, we can accept no more than a cup of coffee. Terrified of what the bathroom scales may tell us, we pick delicately at small portions and shudder at the idea of a second helping. This may not be the diet on which people used to conquer an empire but it does simplify the task of the hostess-cook. On this basis it is just possible for her to play the two parts, vanishing and reappearing as occasion may require. Ingenuity may be needed but the thing can be done.

One problem, however, remains. Shall the ladies retire from the table, leaving the men to drink a glass of port, or should all proceed at once to the drawing room for coffee and cognac? There are two schools of thought about this, and it depends somewhat upon what used to be called the geography of the house. There are physiological reasons, however, for the separation, and something to be said for the port, provided that an alternative is supplied for those whose courage fails. If the proof of a successful party lies in everyone coming to know everyone else, there is reason to segregate the sexes for a while; more especially for men to meet whose conversation has been so far mainly with the ladies. As against this it might be argued that the sexes tend to segregate themselves and that the trend needs no encouragement. Our final conclusion may be that parties vary in their composition and character and that the same rule will not apply to all.

Come now to consider what has become the commoner form of entertainment: the cocktail party, the only way in which we can nowadays invite many people on the same evening. Historically, the cocktail is an aperitif drunk before dinner. It gained prominence under Prohibition in the U.S.A., when wine was banished from the table but when *some* guests, in another room, could have their stimulant unseen by those whose official position or religious views kept them apart. Wine is still more the exception than the rule at the American table, the memory of Prohibition telling in favor of the (far stronger) drinks that are served beforehand. It was soon apparent that the cocktail party could be attended by those who were going to dine elsewhere, becoming thus the subject of a separate invitation. As a final step, the large dinner party became, for most people, impossible; leaving the cocktail party to stand alone.

The Chinese word for cocktail party means, literally, "two-hours-standing-up" and goes, characteristically, to the root of the matter. It is of the essence of such a party that you should stand and circulate. Given an impromptu gathering or an unexpectedly small attendance, the hostess will sometimes find that the chairs suffice for all. "Why don't we sit down?" she asks brightly, and people sink accordingly into her armchairs. The real answer to her question (were we to answer it) is the one nobody could ever give — "Because it will no longer be a cocktail party!" Nor will it, for we all become rooted to the spot by mere politeness. Once seated beside Mrs. A, the man who deliberately rises again after ten minutes is saying to her in everything but words: "I am bored with you and want to talk to that pretty girl by the window."

Worse still, the design of the modern easy chair makes the act of rising a real and visible effort. He must actually struggle to escape, muttering some excuse about not monopolizing the company of Mrs. A. But she, for her part, has no certainty that anyone will take his place. In self-defense she may have to rise as well, making the whole party mobile again. Under conditions of mobility it is easy to extricate oneself from any conversation that has gone on long enough. Talking to Mrs. A, one suddenly catches sight of Colonel B. "Hello, John!" one says with enthusiasm, "haven't seen you for months! Have you been away?" Our enthusiasm over meeting B is our excuse for deserting Mrs. A, who has in any case caught the eye of C, whose common interests with D had been exhausted at about the same time. Standing and circulating may lead to fatigue but there is no other way of managing a cocktail party. In such a party, movement is the first principle and alcohol merely the second.

Our next problem is to decide upon the number of guests. Some hostesses will merely look at their engagement calendar and report that we owe hospitality to seventeen couples, making thirty-four guests, which a normal proportion of refusals would make twenty-eight expected and twenty-four actually there. These, however, are not the best hostesses, their approach being essentially unscientific. Our calculation should begin, rather, with the maximum number our home and parking space can accommodate. This has been established, we shall suppose, by trial and error, giving us a total, shall we say, of eighty. We have next to establish the minimum number for a successful party. To arrive at this figure we must remember, first of all, that the unsuccessful small party is one at which we exhaust our conversation with A, pass on to B, C, D, etc., and then come face to face again with A. The circuit is too small and we tend to remember, after fifty minutes, that we promised to look in on another party. The buzz of conversation begins to falter and there is the sound of cars departing. By eight-ten the host and hostess are alone, saying hopefully to each other, "I *think* that was a success," while knowing, of course, that it was a failure. The guests were too few to entertain each other for as much as an hour and a half.

What, then, is the minimum? Variable factors here are the guests' previous acquaintance with each other, but research results indicate that cocktail party conversations last, on an average, about three minutes. The people who talk for a quarter of an hour with A are usually the very people who dismiss B with a casual greeting as they turn to C. This keeps their average near the norm, and we can safely conclude that we need at least forty guests for a two-hour party. The optimum number must lie, therefore, between forty and eighty.

Can we be more exact? Yes, we can and we must. For if everyone meets everyone else in a party of forty, they must fail to do so in a party that is twice as large. They will end with the feeling that they met only half the other guests and had no more than a formal introduction to the visiting celebrity. This may incline us to suspect that even seventy might be too large. As against that, a total of forty-five would no more than provide for the people who don't *want* to meet each other, either from mutual loathing or from difference in age. The final solution, therefore, is to invite fifty-five people on the assumption that those actually present will number about fifty. And whereas the people well known to each other may reasonably number about forty, the best parties include ten or twelve who are new to the neighborhood or merely there on a visit. Your party should not be just like the last to which you were invited, the same people in a different setting.

The efficient cocktail party demands, ideally, a team of six. These deal, respectively, with the car parking, with the hats and coats, with welcoming the guests, with the drinks, with things to eat and with ensuring that people mix. In practice, these parts may have to be doubled and some even neglected. Where there is proper parking space, guests can sometimes be left to park where they like. The host, who welcomes the guests, may also cope with the raincoats and galoshes — or else, in summer, there may be no problem of this kind. The same person can, just possibly, deal with cheese-straws as well as martinis.

In instances, however, where host and hostess have no assistants, whether co-opted or hired, the hostess welcomes the guests and the host acts as barman. The theory is then that guests can park where they like, put their mink coats on the nearest chair and find, by instinct, where to powder their noses. It is also the theory that the hostess, having welcomed everyone on arrival, is thereafter free to circulate and pass the smoked oysters. It is the unfortunate fact, however, that the last guest arrives only fifteen minutes before the first guest says goodbye.

While the greetings continue at the door, moreover, the most frightful things may be happening among those who arrived earlier. Poor Mrs. X, a widow, is shipwrecked in a corner of the lounge. Mr. and Mrs. Y, newcomers without an acquaintance in the room, are talking to each other in another corner. As for the Bishop of Z, the guest of honor, nobody is talking to him at all. Near the doors opening on the terrace some guest has smashed a tumbler by accident, creating a minefield of broken glass on the carpet. Dr. Alpha, who came early so as to go on to another party, has realized that his sports car is boxed in by Mrs. Omega's station wagon. From the kitchen comes a sinister smell of burning toast and the entrance hall is half blocked by the overcoats which have fallen off a chair. When the last car has gone the host and hostess collapse into chairs with a stiff whiskey apiece. "Well, we did it . . ." they agree, and so in a sense they did. But what was the cost in blood, sweat and tears? Two people have been attempting to do the work of six. Each may have worked as hard as three but this avails them nothing when the tasks are simultaneous. What they were trying to do is not really feasible.

Success in this field of hospitality is to be measured in two ways: first, by the amount of noise, the second, by the lateness of the hour at which people leave. A party composed of the right people in the right number, plied with the right drinks and assisted by blotting paper appetizers at the right intervals, will create a buzz of conversation which rises to its peak some ninety minutes after the party was due to begin. This noise can be measured in decibels, giving a fair indication of the party's relative success. Added to that, however, we have the other test for which only a clock is needed. Should the party begin at six thirty, the last guest should have arrived at seven thirty, the noise should have reached a crescendo by eight and the first goodbye should be said soon afterward. The first departures have no significance, those guests having other engagements for which they are already late.

The crucial test is to observe whether those inevitable farewells trigger off a landslide. If this happens, the last guest leaving at, say, eight fifteen, the party must be judged a relative failure. For one reason or another people were glad to be gone. The really successful party acts like a powerful magnet from which the iron filings must be dragged by force. The early departures are unnoticed and the noise is scarcely diminished at eight fifteen. Some people leave at eight thirty but a number — known technically as the hard core — are still talkative and boisterous at nine, the last group leaving at perhaps nine fifteen. Given this sequence of events the party can be judged a success.

What, however, when the party is more prolonged than that? Some former residents of Singapore may well remember a case in point, a cocktail party held some years ago on the flat roof of a house in Sepoy Lines. The guests may originally have numbered about a hundred (there being no servant problem), and they were mostly there by seven. More than half of them were still there at nine, when food began to appear — chicken legs and curried meat on skewers, Malay fashion — and there was no general exodus until perhaps ten thirty.

The host, a bachelor professor of anatomy, had about him by then a hard core of about a dozen men. So interesting was their conversation that midnight passed unnoticed. With whiskey as their main source of inspiration, they then entered the final (or theological) phase of intoxication. (They were by that time lying on the floor, for technical reasons which we need not discuss.) By 3:00 A.M. they were, naturally, discussing the riddle of the universe. At about 4:10 A.M. they solved it, deciding soon afterward that it was time to go home. Rumor had it next day that our host had concealed a tape recorder behind a Chinese screen and that he now possessed, and was the only possessor of a secret which has baffled mankind since the earliest civilization was founded.

Were this the truth we might fairly conclude that the party was more than justified by results. We would be wrong, however, to argue that the best cocktail parties continue into the small hours, for this was true only of the Far East at a certain period. Without Chinese servants and Malay chauffeurs the situation is entirely different. Lacking this form of support, the host and hostess would wake, hungover, to see about them a scene of seedy squalor. No previous enjoyment could make up for the task which would then await them.

It is this knowledge which underlies the final rule governing this form of entertainment — the rule that everything must be tidy again before the host and hostess go to bed. However distasteful the work may be, it should be done immediately. Never should the morning sun fall pitilessly on a mess of cigar ash and broken glass, empty bottles and chippolata sausage. For any self-respecting household that would be a step toward destruction and doom. To oversleep next day (being Sunday) may be excusable but not so as to allow the wakening eye to rest with nausea on the desolation which remains from the night before. Even if we lack the stamina of our grandparents there is no need for us to be as decadent as that.

CHAPTER SIX

The Children

THE RAISING of a family was once an almost unavoidable result of marriage with only a high infant death rate as a check on overpopulation. In primitive societies children were also regarded as a form of social insurance, the assumption being that they would care for their parents in old age. Nowadays there is a greater element of choice, people being often deliberately childless for a number of years or indeed for life. When pregnancy occurs it is usually as the result of a parental decision, suggesting that the offspring are at least initially wanted.

In thus deciding to have a family the couple concerned have two possible motives. The wife knows that she is capable, as a woman, of two major experiences: marriage and childbirth. To have had both makes her the equal, in this respect, of any other woman, but to have had only the one may leave her dissatisfied; more so, perhaps, than if she has had neither. The husband, for his part, must sympathize with his wife's need for fulfillment, partly from affection and partly from a realization that her discontent would ruin the marriage. He may, however, have his own motives for wishing to have descendants. He may have a family name, inheritance or tradition to perpetuate. This is more obviously true where the family is one of distinction but even more average folk may have a family business or estate with perhaps some obviously inherited streak of ability or skill. For a variety of reasons, some of them intangible, a man may want a son and the more pessimistic may prefer to have several, thus allowing for wastage. As compared with his wife, the man usually looks further ahead, accepting the baby as a present nuisance in order to gain an eventual heir. He may be sensible enough to believe that the son may achieve what the father cannot. He may thus have come to think more of family than of personal goals.

Granted then that children may be desirable, we have next to decide upon their number. All enlightened thought rejects the only child, thus making two the minimum, just insufficient to maintain the population at its present level. A family comprising one boy and one girl might be thought well balanced but with too much reliance on the son's survival. In view of the fact that a single illness or accident might extinguish the family's male line, there is some reason to have a reserve. With that secure most people would regard the family as complete. When it grows larger it is often because daughters predominate, as for example when the second child (and even the third) is a girl, leaving the family with one boy or none. Daughters thus multiply because sons are desired.

The large family of five or more is not, however, generally desirable. While it may offer a good upbringing to the children this is only by a sacrifice of the parents. Five children at an average interval of two years must imply a quarter of a century, more or less, spent in changing diapers and supervising homework. This is justifiable only on the assumption that the children matter more than the parents. But why should this be assumed? There are instances, to be sure, where the fact is evident but the theory that parents should always live for their children is absurd. That the child *might* be an Isaac Newton is true but the father *might* be Johann Sebastian Bach. To conclude that each generation must matter less than the next is manifestly absurd and must lead us nowhere.

The first child tends to appear some two years after the marriage and this arrangement might seem to be the best. For a marriage planned solely for purposes of romantic love will last, on an average, for about two years, ending with the discovery, by one or the other, that someone else is more romantic still. The first child thus arrives rather aptly, adding an element of permanence to a partnership that might otherwise dissolve. There is no current tendency for couples to prolong the childless period but there is, as we have seen, a trend toward early marriage; the result being that few young married folk have had time to develop interests outside the home.

To defer the arrival of the first child would be no remedy, for that would imperil the marriage itself. With a marriage at eighteen and a first child at twenty, the bride of today thus enters a period of twenty to twenty-five years during which her activities will be mainly maternal. If we suppose that this period will end when the youngest child reaches the age of (say) fourteen, the wife and mother will be forty, by the time she is free to relax. It is a late period of life at which to learn another trade and an early age at which to retire. Some may be consoled by the prospect of becoming a grandmother but that is not, or should not be, a full-time occupation for the merely middle-aged.

We might be tempted to remark, at this stage, that life has

its drawbacks from which there is no escape. But this particular problem is of recent origin and is not, in theory, unavoidable. Parents used to delegate their responsibilities to nurses, nursemaids, governesses and tutors. At the lower levels of society children used to be apprenticed at the age of seven or indeed sent to work at the age of five. That parents should be personally responsible for the upbringing of their teen-age children is a twentieth-century concept. One Victorian diarist remarks on the fact that his father spoke to him on only one occasion. Another Victorian complimented a passing nursemaid on the clean appearance of her charges, only to be told that the children — whom he had failed to recognize — were his own. Foster parents were essential to the eigtheenth-century way of life, partly so that children from city homes would be brought up in the country. Ladies still living saw practically nothing of their offspring in childhood and can remember their own parents only as a vague influence over the nursery in which they were themselves brought up. Given a sufficiency of domestic help the mother might see her children for only a few minutes each day while the father might readily avoid seeing them at all. In changed circumstances families are thrown together in a way that people have come to regard as "natural" and with results which no one could have foreseen. What may or may not be of advantage to the children can certainly impose a handicap on the parents. For years at a stretch, for half a lifetime, their daily conversation must be dragged down to the infantile or adolescent level. Their mental growth is thus brought to a standstill.

Few people realize the extent to which our minds are developed (or retarded) by conversation. Our intelligence we may owe to our breeding but its practical usefulness is heightened by debate. We learn from each other by persuasion and argument, by ridicule and reason. Most of all do we learn from contact with men of eminence, from men who have silenced us with their wisdom and wit. And just as our wits are sharpened by such contact so are they blunted by our talk with the prejudiced and dense. With the juvenile and immature our efforts to instruct end in our being drawn down toward their level.

For the sake of illustration, let us assemble a modern family around the supper table. Father has returned from the city to the suburb, the children have returned from school. The family comprises, parents apart, two daughters, Joan and Rachel (aged respectively ten and seven), and one son, Timothy, aged five. The girls attend the same school but Timothy goes to a nursery school within walking distance. A hidden tape recorder bequeathes to posterity the following conversation:

Father: Well, Timothy, what did you learn today in nursery school?
Timothy: Nothing.
Father: What did you do, then?
Timothy: We had baked apples and custard.
Mother: What before that?
Timothy: Sausage and baked beans.
Rachel: That's all that Timothy cares about.
Timothy: I don't! I don't! I hate you!
Mother: Now, now! What about you, Joan?
Joan: We have a new room teacher. She's called Miss Crawley and we all think her fabulous, except that she wears glasses.
Rachel: I'll bet you're aiming to be teacher's favorite!
Joan: I leave *that* to Diana.
Rachel: Who is top in everything, I suppose.

Joan: Not in Art she isn't. Miss Crawley thinks I have real talent.

Rachel: More than you have in Scripture!

Joan: You promised not to tell about that . . .

Rachel: Well, I forgot. It *was* rather funny, though — all that about Esau being a Fairy Man . . .

Joan: Shut up, Rachel! (*screams*) SHUT UP!!

Mother: Not so much noise, children. Did you find your comic, Tim? It was on the kitchen table.

Timothy: Yes, it's super. There's a cat in it called Claudius who can't swim but wants a fish. The pond is like this (*drawing with his finger on the table*), with a fence around *here* and the dog kennel *there* with the bulldog in it called Crusty who hates cats. Claudius has a long, long fishing rod, long as this (*wide gesture*) with a hook on the end, and he whirls it round (*gesture, which upsets Timothy*'s *milk*) . . .

Mother: Fetch a dishcloth and mop it up quickly. (*Order is gradually restored.*)

Rachel: Yours is a silly comic, anyway, fit for babies.

Timothy: It isn't, it isn't! (*cries*).

Mother: You shouldn't have said that, Rachel. It doesn't interest *you* because it is meant for boys, you see. Tim loves it.

Joan: It helps him to lead his gang.

Rachel: He hasn't got a gang.

Timothy: Yes, I have! And my gang always beats the other gang.

Rachel: What other gang?

Timothy: Freddy and Michael. I'll bet you never guess the trick we played on them today.

Joan: You tell us.

Timothy: Well, we dug a great hole, ever so deep, and filled it with water. Then we put leaves and stuff on top so as it looked like grass. When we ran away and they chased us, they all fell in like this — plop — whoosh

— splutter! (*Violent gestures, but Mother has removed his mug in time.*)

Rachel: So you and Teddy dug that big hole in the playground during the morning break?

Joan: Of course they did. Lucky that Miss Medhurst didn't fall into it! (*laughter*).

Rachel: I'll tell you who ought to fall into something, and that's Rosemary.

Joan: Which Rosemary?

Rachel: Rosemary Brent. Our new class captain! Why she should have been chosen I can't think. She's not even clever, although she's so plain and she spends her time cleaning the blackboard.

Joan: You think *you* should have been chosen?

Rachel: Well, why not? I wouldn't have fussed like she does. We all think she's dreary. Sally calls her Nose-Very-Bent!

Joan: I thought we should have to hear about Sally before long.

Rachel: She's my best friend. She wasn't yesterday but now she is again. We are both reading the same story, all about ponies. There's this foal called Prudence and no one thinks she'll ever be any good but Jill loves her very much and trains her in secret. One day Prudence can't be found and they all think she must have been stolen —

Joan: But I'll bet she wins first prize in the end!

Rachel: We haven't got to the end. We are still wondering whether the Gypsies have taken her away to work in a circus or something.

Mother: I daresay it will end happily. We have a choice of pudding today, chocolate mousse or raspberry tart. Who wants which? (*Confusion while each makes the choice, not without changes of mind and a plea from Timothy to have both.*)

Rachel: (*resuming*) One thing about this book is that there are no boys in it, only girls and ponies and a dog called Larry.

Timothy: (*muttering*) My comic has no *girls* in it . . .

Rachel: Jill is mad about show jumping and wants Prudence to win so when she finds the stable empty she feels quite desperate — Sally cried over that bit but I didn't — and her mother tells the police. I wonder if she's really stolen, or just got lost somehow?

Joan: I wouldn't worry too much if I were you.

Timothy: I've finished. Can I get down?

Mother: Wait until the others have finished. Then you can help clear away.

Timothy: Oh, do buck up, everyone!

Mother: Don't be in such a hurry, Tim. I wonder if Daddy wants any more?

Father: Not for me, thanks.

Mother: Then I think we're all finished. Clear the things away, Rachel and Tim, and perhaps Joan will help me in the kitchen. Is there something on television the children will want to see? Let's see, Tuesday, there'll be *The Space Race* at half-past seven for those who have done their homework . . . .

It is the parents' fate to listen, daily, to this sort of conversation; not the talk of the half-witted but that of children who are quite intelligent. As they grow older the children will make amends perhaps by asking questions which may sometimes be a stimulus to thought. In answering them parents may feel compelled to do some quick research at the Public Library. For years, however, the questions are at an elementary level, requiring no more than a simplified answer, and these are the years during which the parents should have progressed. The mother is the prime victim but it would be wrong to think that the father does not suffer at all. For while his wife is dragged down to the children's level of conversation, he is dragged down to hers. By middle age they may be left without an idea in their heads.

Mental development or the lack of it can be roughly measured by the literature to be found in the home. If there are no books we may conclude, perhaps, that there was nothing much to develop. More often, the books represent our phases of growth. An average home may thus contain, first of all, the books which father studied when qualifying as, say, a public accountant. To these may be added a few more recent editions in the same field, sometimes with the leaves unopened. If mother was once a student of home economics, her textbooks will also be there with one or two more recent works on cookery. Three or four volumes of poetry reflect a passing phase of her early married life and a Spanish phrase book reminds her of the year they actually went to Andalusia or Mexico. To judge from the dates of publication, no further books were acquired for some years, save perhaps on gardening or carpentry. Then we have the books for children, including a dictionary, an atlas, and the children's encyclopedia to which the young can be referred on what the parents have forgotten or else have never known. Last of all we have the paperbacks, picked up in the course of travel, mostly thrillers, to which may be added a few odd numbers of *Reader's Digest*. That would be the showing of an average middle-class household and the story it has to tell is of mental growth arrested as from the birth of the first child. There is no evidence of developing interests or changes in taste, no signs of enthusiasm for drama or history, for science or current affairs. Any knowledge the parents may have was gained in school or college. There is no indication that they are interested in antiques or sculpture, in religion or ballet. They have ceased to grow, it would seem, as from the time when they began to breed.

Is this an overstatement of the case? We may argue, if we will, that the parents can become mentally active after the children have been put to bed. Given a baby-sitter, they can go to the concert or attend a repertory cinema, engage in politics or make a collection of stamps. All these possibilities exist, but they remain for most people no more than possible. The fact would seem to be that the average mother is exhausted by evening and the average father scarcely less so. The unfortunate result is that they have the less to offer their adolescent children. Having given time and energy to the very young, they have no discoveries to share with the same children when older.

To write off the children and turn to other things may seem a cold-hearted procedure but of one thing we can be sure and that is that those who will most obviously benefit are the children themselves. For their contact in adolescence will be with parents who are themselves growing and developing. Instead of a mother who droops over the photograph album and points out how sweet Julia looked at the age of three, the children will have someone more interesting to whom they can turn; a woman with ideas and new activities, and one who is not merely obsessed with motherhood.

Given the choice, we know perfectly well what the children both need and prefer. Granted that they want parents on whose kindness they can rely, they do not want parents who rely in turn on their children for company. Of all things to be avoided is the attitude of those who say (in everything but words), "We looked after you when you were young — gave up our lives to you, denied you nothing. Now we are old and the least you can do is to spare some time for your Mum and Dad. It is not asking much." But parents should never allow themselves to become dependent upon their children, least of all for affection. The process by which parents are dragged down to the nursery level of conversation must recoil, in the end, on the children themselves. Failing to develop, the mother and father are left behind by the children themselves and are mentally deprived by the time the children have gone.

All that is left for the child-oriented parent is the prospect of becoming a grandparent. This is merely an opportunity to make the same mistake again. It is true that a grandmother is sometimes the answer to the baby-sitter problem but this hardly justifies her in making baby-sitting a career. For the sad fact is that marrying early has changed the pattern of grandmaternity. The girl who marries at eighteen may be no more than thirty-seven when her daughter acts as hastily. A grandmother of thirty-eight may fill that role for another thirty years or more. This is a monstrous period of time to spend in offering unwanted advice to daughters and daughters-in-law. The only solution is to be less obsessed with children from the outset.

Osborn

CHAPTER SEVEN

Mrs. Parkinson's Law

THIS CHAPTER is specifically intended for the married woman whose children are of school age; the woman for whom life often becomes too much. This does not mean, however, that her husband should omit this chapter, for he needs, surely, to know what her problems are. Central to them is the periodic impact of the day of crisis, the moment of grief, the hour when the world seems about to end. Black disaster threatens on every side and you (the housewife) do not know whether to scream, to pray or to put your head in the gas oven. In studying this situation, let us see it, first of all, from the outside. Suppose, in the first instance, that it is someone else who is in trouble; an acquaintance and neighbor, a woman known to you as respectable and harmless, one who lives a little way down the street and on the opposite side. Suppose, further, that she is called (say) Yardley, the wife of a bank executive. Looking casually out of your front window, you realize that something has gone wrong.

Yes, there is something amiss in the Yardleys' home and the goldfish-bowl nature of the modern suburb allows you to share in it. With picture windows and open plan, with flimsy walls and grass lawn, our more modern houses hold few secrets from each other. When the Bronowskis at 2034 are giving a party, the fact is apparent to all who were not invited. When the Schuylers at 2031 are having a quarrel the cause of the dispute becomes instantly known to all within a hundred yards. In the present instance there is no family dispute and none expected — for the Yardleys are an amicable couple — but Gwen is clearly upset. Her voice is raised, and so, on a higher pitch, is that of her only child (Buster, aged four).

There is a man at her front door and you recognize him as the pollster who called yesterday on you. He is distributing some questionnaire in which opinions are canvassed about nuclear warfare. "Ma-m-may I approach you," he began, "as a leader of op, op, opinion in this neighborhood. . . ." Gwen has flung open the door and is listening to what must be his standard opening. Even at this distance you can appreciate that she is registering a sense of suppressed fury. You are not one to pry into your neighbors' troubles (heaven knows you have other things to do), but something of tension in the scene keeps you glued to the window. The little man is explaining, no doubt, that the world — without Gwen's intervention — is doomed. Gwen's hostility projects itself successfully the length of the block.

Suddenly there comes an explosion of almost nuclear violence. The words "GET OUT!!!" are all you actually hear, but Gwen's torrent of screamed abuse is easily imaginable. The questionnaire is being torn into shreds. The terrified pollster is stumbling down the path. He has tripped and fallen on the sidewalk, scattering literature as he runs toward his car, and a minute later he and it have vanished and Gwen stops shaking her fist. Her glass-topped door slams and there is the sound of broken glass. More faintly comes the slam of an inner door, Buster's wail and the crash of disintegrating chinaware. For Gwen, poor girl, it is evidently one of those days when *everything goes wrong.*

Do you yourself have such days of disaster? You do? How do they begin, then, and what is the sequence of events? Are they avoidable? You may have concluded that they are a feature of an ill-planned universe and that there is nothing you can do about it. In this you may well be mistaken. As diagnosis comes before treatment, our first step must be to reconstruct the crisis. This we have often seen done by television detectives. "Put the furniture back where it was, open the window, switch off the standard light. Sit in the armchair, Watson. Now, I will enter by the door as the murderer must have done. . . . What do I see? Nothing. Why not? Because the room is in pitch darkness!" "Holmes, this is marvelous!" The same technique can be applied to our own less melodramatic affairs.

Let us begin, then, with an imaginary situation of which you might well be the victim. Your husband and children have gone respectively to office and school and the day, we shall suppose, is cold, foggy and wet. With the mail comes a letter from the downtown department store, regretting that the dressing table you wanted, an antique, has been sold cheaply to someone else. You learn by telephone that your plan for the vacation has fallen through, the hotel having been wrecked by an avalanche. The agent assures you that it is now too late to book accommodation elsewhere. Marty's school report arrives, and you tear it open, glimpsing the words "untidy" and "idle." The toaster jams, filling the kitchen with black smoke. The coffee saucepan boils over on the stove. You break a decorative and valuable piece of china, the Royal Worcester plate on which you serve the cookies. Everything, but *everything* is against you. All evidence points to the existence of a conspiracy, which might be defined in scientific terms as the inveterate malignancy of inanimate objects. You relieve your feelings by canceling a hair appointment, complaining by telephone about your neighbor's dog and kicking a Jehovah's Witness off the doorstep. You end with a minor car accident and a parking ticket.

Why does all this have to happen to us? Why this sequence of dilemma, disaster and dismay? Under emotional stress, we ask these questions of an unresponsive heaven, being unable to provide the answers for ourselves. But *now,* as you read this, you are cool and collected and can realize that your sequence of events is not a sequence at all. The successive tragedies are unrelated and fall, in any case, into two separate groups. The bargain is lost, the vacation plan spoiled and the school report received; all these incidents are *external* and beyond your control. The toaster, the saucepan and the china plate are *internal* disasters and strictly your own doing. Study the apparent sequence afresh. The loss of the bargain is bad luck and there is nothing you can do about it — save to note that you have some extra money for the replanned vacation. You might say that the hotel cancellation is purely disastrous; but is it? After all, the avalanche might have happened while you were there, and even while you were in the bath. You are well out of it in that sense. Now, look at the report again. How does it go? "Although Marty is sometimes rather untidy, he is never ill-behaved or idle and his work shows definite signs of improvement." Not so bad, really, and better anyway than the last.

The other disasters were all (let's face it) your own doing. The toaster and coffee went wrong because you were thinking about the dressing table, not about the task in hand. But the breaking of the china plate represents something more complex. Women express their annoyance in the first place by rattling dishes and slamming doors. Dishes are apt to break when rattled. Broken to fragments and slammed into the trash can, they also serve as a protest against the unfairness of the world. The odd plate or saucer would mean no more than that, but the breaking of Royal Worcester or Spode is something different. It reveals that you are behaving childishly, that you *know* your behavior is childish, that you are punishing yourself like a child and using a childish form of punishment.

But your annoyance does not stop there. Why should it, and indeed how can it? You go on to punish yourself and others until such time as you recover. It is only then, hours (or days) later, that you study the situation afresh and find that it is not so serious after all. Until that moment of calm you will continue to exemplify the Second Law of Thermodynamics: the law that heat energy is always transferred from a body with a higher temperature to one with a lower temperature; in this instance from you to the Jehovah's Witness, stunned with a blow from your frying pan. There can be no such transfer, however, unless there is another body there to receive it. In this instance your heat energy was distributed between the hairdresser, the neighbor's dog and the evangelist; which was fortunate for the last, who might otherwise have been killed outright.

It is obvious that your generated and transferable heat is potentially dangerous and may lead to results which escalate (a good contemporary expression) from slander to assault and from divorce to murder. To lessen this danger, as we plainly must, we have to decide (1) how the heat generates and whether it need be generated at all, and (2) if it has to generate, how it can be dispersed harmlessly before any real mischief has been done? The clue to (1) lies in the First Law of Thermodynamics: the law that heat is absorbed in proportion to the work done under pressure, a given quantity of work producing a definite equivalent of heat. This law applies to the emotional as well as to the physical temperature.

Household work is apt to be done under pressure because it fluctuates, rising to a peak (for example) when packing the children off to school, and rising to another peak as the guests are due to arrive in the evening. The heat is apt to remain after its immediate causes have gone, building up at successive peaks until the explosion occurs — a nuclear accelerator works in somewhat the same way. But *why* does the heat build up? Why is it not dissipated between the periods of domestic crisis? After years of experiment, at the cost of thousands ($782.95 in crockery alone), we have finally solved this apparently insoluble problem. And here in twelve words is the answer: *Because you have nobody else to whom your heat can be transferred.*

It all goes back to a song entitled *Tea for Two* which included the following significant lines:

> Tea for two and two for tea
> Me for you and you for me. . . .
> Don't you see how happy we will be?

Reading between the lines, we conclude from this that the couple are to be alone together; which you may think normal. This plan is peculiar, however, to the twentieth century and peculiar to the West. In any previous century and in almost any part of the world, your household could have been organized on very different lines. The old-fashioned or Oriental family comprised relatives, children, servants and friends. In Imperial Rome there would have been adherents and parasites, eunuchs and concubines, bodyguards, astrologers, slave girls and slaves. Even in relatively modern India the seventh Grand Nizam of Hyderabad had a thousand servants to staff his principal palace, with three thousand guardsmen and four thousand more employees on other estates.

In other words, there were other people around. Given the day of apparent disaster you would have someone to blame, someone who would sympathize and someone again who would probably laugh. Your heat would then transfer itself to cooler minds and, the initial disasters being forgotten, the later disasters would not have occurred. All you ever had, by contrast, was tea for two and two for tea. With your husband at the office, you are alone in the house, with the telephone your only hope. That instrument is your only "ground" in the electrical sense, the lightning conductor which will convey some of your emotions out of the house. This accounts for your fury when the line is busy or when nobody replies. Solitude, in short, has its drawbacks. And the rhetorical question, "Don't you see how happy we will be?" may suggest the answer, "Well, actually, I *don't.*"

Research has now established the fact that the day of domestic disaster is due to stress caused by a heat for which there is no sufficient outlet. More than that, we can put this into precise and scientific language. Mrs. Parkinson's Law, as it is called, applying to the married woman of the Western world, runs thus:

HEAT PRODUCED BY PRESSURE
EXPANDS TO FILL THE MIND AVAILABLE
FROM WHICH IT CAN PASS ONLY
TO A COOLER MIND

This discovery, momentous as it is, must fail of its maximum impact if not also stated in mathematical terms. For this purpose the first tentative formula was submitted to the world's greatest authority on domestic thermodynamics, Professor Darcy C. Coyle of the Rensselaer Polytechnic Institute of Connecticut, Inc., a copy of whose first tentative reply was accidentally enclosed in some mail addressed to that Institute's Bureau of Research. This Bureau took automatic action as a result of which copies in quintuplicate were passed to ten federal agencies in Washington, D.C. Rather to his surprise (for he had made no application) Professor Coyle promptly received a grant of $166,276, including $151,116 for overhead and paperwork.

Thus encouraged, he made a series of field surveys for empirical data and several emergency visits to the hospitals of Connecticut. All results were then fed into an IBM 360 Computer, which then produced the following equation:

$$T_D = .052\,(W\sqrt{S+N} - W\sqrt{s+n})$$

where T_D = the emotional temperature differential,
W = the weight of the housewife in pounds,
S = her speed in mph, and
N = number of crises encountered by the housewife within the past six hours.

Of course, w, s and n stand for the weight, speed and crises involving another person encountered by the housewife while in orbit.*

Commenting upon these calculations, Professor Darcy Coyle states his opinion that any differential greater than plus or minus 5 is dangerous. He adds, however, that substantial testing of a very destructive type would be necessary

* It should be noted, incidentally, that the emotional temperature of any human is now contained in the formula: $T_H = .52\,W\sqrt{S+N}$

to determine this safety range between two sigma limits of certainty. He suggests that there may be a far more dangerous point where $T_D = 0$ but W and w are equally great and S and s are equally fast. This could be a point of destruction in both directions, and a formula, in effect, for a nuclear explosion. Without further experiment (and probable casualties) there can, of course, be no certainty about this. Granted the desirability of research on these lines, there seems no point in any secrecy about the result so far obtained. In all its grand simplicity, the first mathematical statement of Mrs. Parkinson's Law is now offered to the world.

This first result, impressive as it is, was thought, however, to be insufficiently complex and the same data was fed into a more expensive computer. The new result, a definite advance, reads thus:

$$T_d = .37\,(WS - ws) + 2\,(N - n) - \frac{45}{1 + N - n}$$

where W is the housewife's weight in pounds, S is her speed in miles per hour, N is the number of disasters occurring to her, and w, s and n are weight, speed and number of crises occurring to another person just prior to contacting her. T_d is the emotional temperature differential; as long as it is positive, our heroine will tend to explode at the other person, but when it becomes negative, her own health may suffer.

If we translate this into the figures which might relate to a specific case, allowing the housewife a weight of 133.24 pounds and a crisis-free speed of 2 mph, her emotional temperature under ideal conditions would read as follows:

$T_H = .37\ (133.24)\ 2 = 98.57°F$, practically normal. If we assume, however, that she speeds up to 3 mph and has one crisis just before she contacts another person who weighs 130 pounds who is going 2½ mph without any problems, then we have:

$$T_d = .37\ (133.24 \times 3 - 130 \times 2\tfrac{1}{2}) + 2\ (1 - 0)\ \frac{45}{1 + 1 - 0}$$
$$= .37\ (399.72 - 325) + 2 - 22.5$$
$$= 27.65 + 2 - 22.5 = +7.15$$

Again, if the housewife weights exactly 134.08 pounds and moves at 2 mph without any crisis, we have $T_H = .52\ (134.08)\sqrt{2} = 98.601°$ Fahrenheit, only a bit over normal. However, at this same weight, but moving at 5.25 mph after 4 crises, her emotional temperature becomes

$T_H = .52\ (134.08)\sqrt{5.25 + 4} = 212.050°F$, somewhat over the boiling point. On the other hand, men of passionate nature should avoid women weighing less than 102.56 pounds who move at a speed under .36 mph because

$T_H = .52\ (102.56)\sqrt{.36} = 32.000°F$, or freezing, and this can be extremely dangerous regardless of T_D, the emotional temperature differential.

At this point the research fund was exhausted. While it may be true that further work at a higher cost would yield a more elaborate equation, the present result would seem quite sufficient for all practical purposes. Until superseded the present formula can be inscribed on granite in letters of gold.

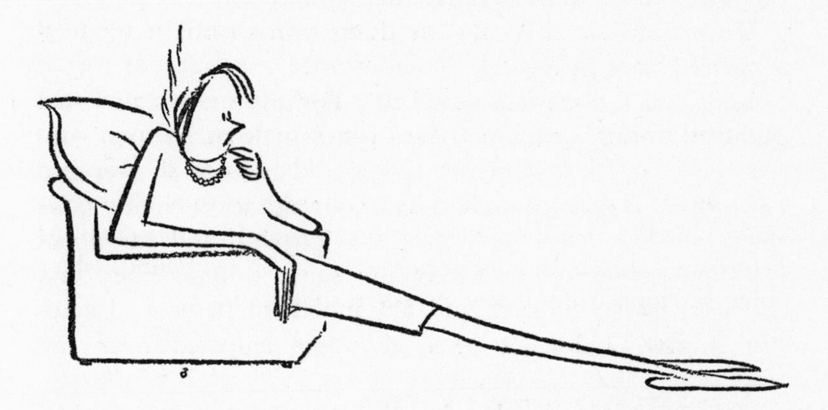

We know now the process by which our heat is generated. We also know the circumstances in which it fails to disperse, building up to the point of explosion. This brings us to the two practical questions: How can we stop the process of generation? Failing that, how can we disperse the heat we have generated? Toward checking the rise in temperature, the first step is to know Mrs. Parkinson's Law and realize that you are subject to it. The second step is to recognize the symptoms of stress and apply the following rules: First, never look at the incoming mail until you have time to read it at leisure. A quick glance will often leave you with the wrong impression, worrying about some problem which may not even exist. Remember, therefore, that there is no special urgency about a piece of paper. It can wait and it probably should. Your better policy is to concentrate on what you are doing. Second, never answer the telephone if you are in the middle of something more important. Let it ring. If the caller has any message of consequence she will ring again. Third, when disaster strikes as the result of your own agitation, stop work, switch off, sit down, collect your thoughts and pull yourself together. Do nothing more until your temperature is normal.

Are these three rules sufficient? For the more emotional they are probably not. So there is a fourth rule which runs as follows: In the last resort take a cold bath or shower and emerge in a cooler frame of mind, your agitation having gone down the drain pipe. It is true that physical and emotional temperatures are not exactly the same thing. They are, however, closely related, and few moods of panic will actually survive a bucket of cold water emptied over the head.

The point of this drastic measure, were it practicable, would be to lower the temperature and at the same time break the sequence of disaster. With something else to think about, the cold shock, the effort of drying herself, the housewife would eventually return to her work in a different mood. Once she has realized that the root of the trouble is in herself, not in a conspiracy of people and things, she is on the way to recovery. It would be wrong, incidentally, to conclude that men never yield to panic and ill-temper when things go wrong. They do so more rarely when at work, for few of them work entirely alone, but they are not invulnerable when at home.

Given some task like mowing the lawn, papering the bathroom or pruning the roses (while the wife is out shopping),

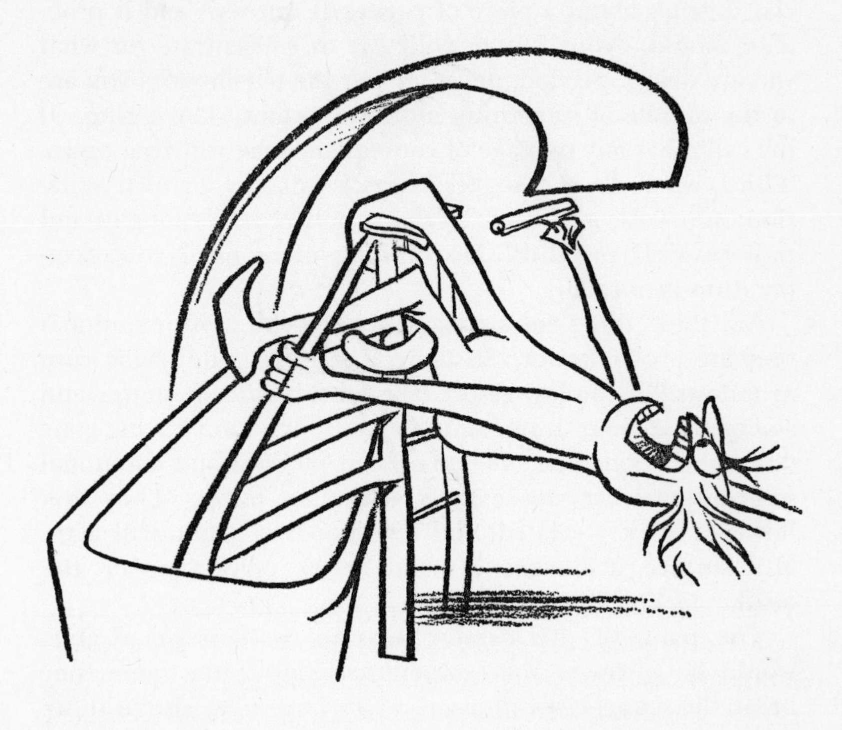

the husband can equally fall a victim to Mrs. Parkinson's Law. He too can feel that everything is against him, that disasters have befallen and that a still worse disaster is probably on its way. The rules to obey in such a situation are exactly the same as laid down for the housewife, with the single addition that he should afterward light his pipe. Stop work, switch off, sit down and, if necessary, take a cold shower.

Sound as far as they go, these rules which should be infallible so far as the husband is concerned may be insufficient

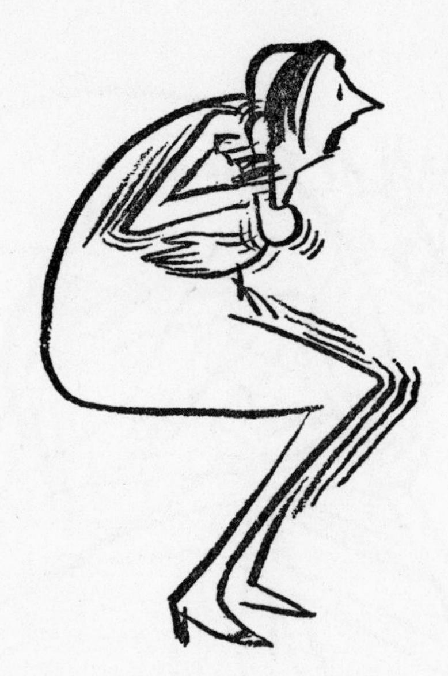

to save the housewife. She is more vulnerable, perhaps, more prone to moods of despair. Events can happen too quickly, moreover, each calamity overtaking the last. Despite all our efforts, the situation can get out of hand. You find yourself disobeying rules (1) and (3). Let us suppose, in fact, that the sequence of events is very much that described earlier in this chapter and that heat remains *after* the incident on the doorstep. Your favorite piece of china is in fragments. You have burned your best dress with the iron. You have seen the Jehovah's Witness taken to the hospital. You are all a-tremble, wondering what fresh catastrophe will follow. You seem to be on a collision course with Destiny.

Were you ignorant of Mrs. Parkinson's Law — as you were until a few minutes ago — your instinct would be to call your husband at the office. Grabbing the telephone and get-

ting his extension, you would begin to babble your grief with emotional incoherence. "It's-terrible-darling-I-only-wanted-him-to-go-away-but-there-he-was-stunned-and-the-ambulance-came-and-everything-my-best-dress-ruined-and-the-china-broken-if-only-everything-didn't-happen-at-once-I-could-cope-but-its-utter-hell-and-what-shall-I-do?" A message of this urgency will normally find your husband in one of two situations. He may be in conference, fighting for dear life against some idiotic scheme which threatens to wreck his whole career. He may, alternatively, be working quietly at his desk. In the one case his reply may be almost as agitated as your appeal for help: "For Pete's-sake-I'm-in-conference-it's-all-I-can-do-to-hold-my-own-the-stupid-ideas-some-people-have-My-God-and-now-you-have-to-start-screaming-about-broken-china. Hang-up-like-a-good-girl-and-take-a-couple-of-aspirins-I'll-get-home-early-if-I-can-g'bye." In the other

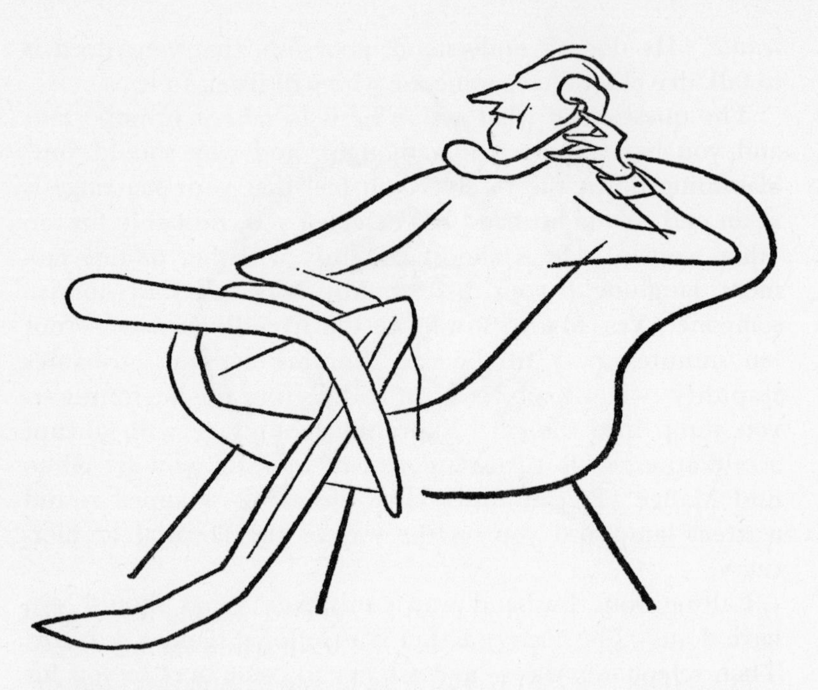

event he will be perfectly and maddeningly sensible. "Don't you think, darling, that you should tell me in simple words, what you want me to *do?* Why don't I call you back in ten minutes so that you can decide by then what help you want? Hang up, baby, and calm down. Then tell me how I can help. G'bye for now."

Of these two possible types of response the second is the more fatal. The first admittedly gets you nowhere but it suggests that you are not alone: he too has his troubles. The second lacks even that crumb of comfort. What you are seeking is a "ground" into which your heat can discharge itself. While cool enough for that purpose, your husband refuses to cooperate. Instead of listening to your incoherent drivel, he cuts through it and comes to the point — "what do you *want?*" He doesn't understand, poor fish, that your need is to talk drivel and have someone who will listen to it.

The question of what *action* he is to take is unimportant and you haven't given it a thought, and why should you? Slamming down the receiver you feel that your marriage is at an end. Your husband has deserted you, probably for another woman. He is almost certainly with her at this moment, laughing at your distress. You *must* tell your story to someone! Yes, Madge would be the friend you need — not ten minutes away in the car. Fuming at your husband's stupidity — it was all *his* fault, really, from the beginning — you jump into the car. Expressing your rage with abrupt acceleration, wide turns and violent braking, you set off to find Madge. Five minutes later the car is wrapped round a street lamp and you on the way to the hospital or mortuary.

Calling your husband was a mistake. What should you have done? The correct action is as follows: Take a sedative. Then telephone Madge and ask *her* to come over to you for coffee, not immediately but in half an hour's time. Then sit down (very important, this) and write a brief report on the events which have disturbed you. Don't attempt to make any decisions. Decide, rather, not to decide for the present. Wait until you have further information or advice, putting problems out of your mind until you have time to deal with them. By the time your friend arrives, you will have begun to cool. By the time you have told her the story, you should be back to normal. Having told your story and received some sympathy, and having shelved the practical problems until tomorrow, do the minimum of what has to be done and then settle down with an extremely unexciting book. What book? Why, this one, of course. And which chapter? The chapter you have just finished.

CHAPTER EIGHT

Aims and Objects

WHEN THE LAST CHILD has reached school age, the moment has come for the parents to decide, perhaps belatedly, what they are trying to do. They have made, let us assume, some initial effort to escape from failure and poverty. They have been driven into romance by their sexual needs and by the conventions of the society into which they have been born. Falling in love, they have married; and this process implies (they find) a home, a car and facilities for entertaining. To promote the wife's sense of fulfillment and continue the family name, children have been bred and are now being educated.

If the sole object in all this were to replace the parents by children whose lives are to be the same, the repetition would seem pointless. Why should a stockbroker spend his life in providing the community with a physiotherapist and a public accountant? Why should the public accountant then exhaust himself in producing another stockbroker? Doubling the population does no more than create a worse traffic problem.

What, then, is the object of the exercise? There are people who argue hopefully that the children should be better than the parents, each generation more admirable than the last.

and that this is the sort of progress we should seek to bring about. We have no evidence, however, that the children are an improvement on their ancestors. In one way, moreover, they are apt to be inferior, for the children of successful parents are without the spur of poverty. They have never made the effort to fight their way out of the slum. Finding it relatively easy to remain in the income group to which they belonged from birth, they have little incentive to make any effort of any kind.

They may be healthier than their grandparents were and they are probably taller, but greater size does not imply greater vitality. We may suspect, indeed, that larger folk waste their energy in merely propelling their additional weight. The idea that the world improves itself has to be discarded. That we could improve it ourselves is possibly true but we cannot do so by breeding bigger children with smaller incentives. Whatever is to be done is for us to do.

What, however is our object to be? We can try to serve God or Mankind, or at least the community in which we live. We can seek wealth or status, power or happiness, pleasure or escape. We can even strive, if we will, to achieve mere security in our old age. While this last aim may be reasonable, at least up to a point, we can dismiss it at once as an object for which to live. Age should be no more the object of youth than youth should be the object of age. We should not live to earn a pension any more than we should wake in order to sleep. Granted that some measure of security may be desirable, we ought surely to achieve more in life than that.

What, for instance, if we were to make wealth our object? Here is an aim which a majority of people would reject, no doubt, with scorn. Among the most scornful are those who are incapable of earning or saving more than will keep them alive. How many who could actually make money have refrained from doing so? And were they in any case right to refrain? Making a fortune is a more harmless activity than many people imagine, but it does invite the further question as to what the money is for. In all common sense it can be no more than a means to an end.

What is the millionaire to do when his millions are made? He can buy political power for himself or his sons or else buy the politicians among whom the power is divided. He can buy the symbols of status in countries where status is still symbolized. He can buy food, drink, sex, company and comfort. He can finally buy escape, the South Sea Island where all is sunshine, beauty and peace. But most pleasures show a diminishing return in terms of enjoyment. A sufficiency can be obtained without being wealthy and an excess leads only to indigestion, illness and fatigue. The person who lives for pleasure is like the blind man in the dark room looking for a black cat that is not there. By the very nature of things he is doomed to disappointment.

The problem for the individual is hardly less of a problem for the community. There were once principalities and cities which served a definable purpose. They were there to uphold an ideal or defend a faith. Greek cities were so designed as to illustrate the Greek view of life. Roman cities expressed the Roman sense of discipline and order. Crusader castles breathed defiance against Islam and medieval cities vied with each other in the size and splendor of their churches.

In many places and periods it was possible to see at a glance what a community was trying to do. This is possible now only in communities which are devoted to the preservation of something which exists. For cities of fairly recent origin express no ideal save that of making money in the congestion of the center and spending it on the comfort of the suburbs. What communal efforts are made are mostly negative, groups thus demanding the clearance of slums or the improvement of hospitals. People will agree that tension may be reduced if poverty is relieved. Efforts are thus made to provide recreation for the young or accommodation for the old.

All such activities should, however, be marginal to the main effort and no such effort has been planned. There are groups and families which can point with pride to a concert hall or library. There are individuals who can claim credit for a smokeless zone or a project of urban renewal. There are few instances, however, of a whole community sharing in some positive achievement. It is nevertheless in such a communal effort that individuals probably find their greatest happiness. Losing themselves in a common cause they can forget their grievances and cease to notice their discomforts and ailments. Without an aim in common they must find that any communal happiness is unattainable.

Family ambitions remain and success in this area can be measured in terms of wealth or status. Large-scale wealth is not normally within the grasp of the middle-class family. Given security and comfort, few people will hazard all they possess on a gambler's chance of the jackpot. In the first place, they feel too responsible for their family's welfare. In the second place, they are unconvinced that a vast increase of fortune would bring them a proportionate satisfaction. It is only people in the lowest class who generate the drive which will earn them a fortune, for they start with a savage determination to escape from poverty, and start moreover

with nothing to lose. Of any ten such upstarts nine will end in prison and the tenth will be a millionaire. Very few millionaires have a cozy middle-class background and fewer still are graduates of the business school.

Among the trained and qualified folk of the modern suburb, the aim is to leave their children more prosperous still with higher salaries and influential friends. All this falls far short of real wealth, the effect of inheritance being to reduce incentive and impose caution. Who are we to gamble with grandfather's hard-earned capital? We think of it, rather, as something held in trust for our children, a safeguard for our unmarried daughters or a pittance for our more shiftless sons.

Wealth, then, for most of us, is not the object of existence. But status remains the goal for many in societies which are sufficiently stratified and which thus offer reward in terms of status. "Snobbish" is the word which comes to mind and we at once recall the sort of monologue in which the elderly wife and grandmother will indicate the values which she has come to regard as sacred. Let us place her in the rose garden and listen respectfully to her comments upon weeping standards and hybrid teas:

"Until this year my favorite was the Grace de Monaco — she chose it herself, you know, such a delicate shade of silvery pink — but I am prouder now of the miniatures, Perle de Montserrat, and, above all, the Diane Radziwill. Sheer sentiment, I suppose — she planted this one herself in those happier days when John was still alive. But some people think the color is too vivid. My brother, Mark, *will* call it 'brick red' but you know how difficult it is to please *him*. Are all Admirals like that? I expect they are. It always seems to me that Generals have more tact. I know my uncle

Ned always said the right thing to everybody. But *he* would never have thought it possible to grow roses without horse manure. Did you ever see the stables at Canterley Court? There must have been twenty hunters in the old days and the roses really *thrived!* Scientists tell us that these chemical fertilizers are just as good, but dear Harold (I don't mean the *present* P.M.!) would never believe it. He and Derek were at school together, you know, and served in the same Regiment. But World War I is ancient history now! They didn't agree, by the way, on anything except gardening. I hope I'm not boring you about the roses? Are you sure? I showed two visitors around last week and did a sort of Ruth Draper act, talking for hours before I discovered that the Bishop is color-blind and the Judge has no sense of smell! They were terribly nice about it, though, much nicer than Evelyn Waugh would have been. I am terrified of authors, aren't you? I always think that they will put one into the next novel. You might think that fear absurd, with me such a nobody, but one of them actually did! The book was a flop, though, which is just as well. My grandchildren would have found a best seller terribly embarrassing and everyone else at Trinity or Christ Church would have read it. . . . The beech hedge has grown up well, hasn't it? It helps to hide the cottage built by some rather ghastly people who have come to live here — folk from Huddersfield, I'm told, or some such place. . . . We had a tragedy here in this corner. I planted a sequoia here, one of the giant trees from California. They take eight hundred years to mature, but this one failed to last as many seconds. It was dug up by Derek's corgi, Vestal the Third. She afterward won her class at Cruft's but it was no real consolation. Well, here we are back on the terrace and you have earned a drink. What shall it be? Black Velvet or Blanc de Blanc?"

In this one speech are crowded, rather breathlessly, all or most of the status symbols which constitute the lady's background. Even if she were lying, they would still represent the values in which she believes. Her artless chatter is designed, first of all, to establish that she comes from the country not from the town. She has known from childhood about soil and trees, about flowers and shrubs. She is casually familiar (she hints) with people in the highest society, but she is too well established among the in-group to make it a subject for boasting. She is interested not so much in politics as in horses and dogs. Her relatives and friends hold high rank in the Navy and Army, the Church and the Law. Her husband is an old Etonian who served at one time in the Brigade of Guards.

But she herself is mildly intellectual, knowing something perhaps of literature and the stage. Her aim in this monologue is to establish her own status; proof in itself that her position is more on the fringe than in the center. While her consequent insecurity is manifest, there is some basis for her claim to social consequence. It is at least equally clear that she is a very silly woman indeed.

While her folly must be admitted, however, her values are not entirely false. She is not suggesting that her friends are all colossally wealthy. She is not even hinting that she has influence. She merely wants to emphasize her "County status," her relationships and friendships among people of good family and professional standing. She likes it to be known that members of her family have a gallant record and have risen, some of them, to high command. In all this there is ground for legitimate pride. She may be stupid to talk about it, but we would be wrong, surely, to grudge her the satisfaction of basking in reflected glory. She is at least admiring the right people for more or less the right reasons. Her heroes have reached some sort of eminence in their calling. There are other people who admire less honorable acquaintances for less creditable achievements.

Status, then, is something for which we may strive and the effort to gain it is a part of the total dynamics of society. The same can hardly be said of the quest for happiness as opposed to pleasure and it may be questioned, indeed, whether happiness is ever achieved by those who make it their object. Insofar, however, as it is attainable it is attained by simplifying one's wants. The symbol of happiness is the log cabin on the island, the simple diet and the outdoor life. Fleeing from civilization, we might discard the automobile and the radio, reduce our belongings to the minimum, and commune henceforth with the beauties of nature. So far as our later years are concerned there might be something in this idea. Earlier in life the plan would break down, however, over the children's upbringing. It is one thing to go into the wilderness with a well-stocked mind and the memory of a thousand books, quite another to breed children who have never seen a library, concert hall or theater. Whether they would be happy is doubtful and the likelihood is that they would revert to a kind of savagery which might be very unpleasant indeed. One does not achieve the primitive by rebelling against civilization. There is a lesson to be learned from William Golding's *Lord of the Flies*; the lesson that, even going to a desert island, we take our corruption with us.

What, then, are we trying to do? We are not merely perpetuating the species. Only to a minor extent are we serving the community or mankind. Wealth is for most of us unattainable and we doubt, incidentally, whether it is worth pursuing. Status is perhaps more valuable but the effort to secure it can easily become absurd. Like happiness it usually comes as a by-product of something else. There are physical limits to the pleasure we can buy and mere security can hardly be an end in itself.

What, then, is our object to be? The answer for most sensible people is to find a balance between all these possible motives but with a shift in emphasis from time to time, perhaps when opportunity offers, and more often when circumstances change. To think only of money is to become a miser and therefore miserable. To dream only of status is to make oneself ridiculous. To live for one's children is almost as pointless as it would be for our children to live for their parents. The search for happiness can end unhappily and the craze for pleasure will make us sick. What we need above all is a sense of proportion. This truth is central to the civilization we have inherited and all our experience goes to prove it. Without a sense of balance we are lost.

In all this comparison of the possible objects for which we may strive, we have left out, so far, the one that probably matters most of all. This is the urge to create something of beauty, value and interest. The artist, author or musician is pursuing an object which is neither (directly) status, wealth, happiness nor security. The sculptor who carves a masterpiece out of rock is creating a thing of beauty. In doing so he has combined work with play, grudging the time he must spend upon meals and sleep. The resulting statue may bring him a sum of money and a higher reputation in the world of art. He will have been happy while working and is satisfied with the work when complete. His fame, he believes, will outlive him, his best work remaining as a legacy to future generations.

He can thus have the fun and pocket the fee, a privilege

he shares with the composer or dramatist, painter or poet. It is only in this sort of career that all or most of the possible aims can be reconciled and unified. There can hardly be a greater satisfaction in life than composing the music for a successful musical comedy. To set the whole world singing must be happiness enough in itself, but to amuse oneself in the process and gather fame and fortune as a result is to have nearly all at once of what life can offer. This is the great artist's privilege and one for which few of us will ever qualify. What we forget, however, is that we can do something comparable at a lower level.

Without any genius of our own, without anything more than ability and common sense, we can share in the efforts and rewards of creativity. We can play some part in the making of something useful and beautiful, adding our signature with a flourish. Great works of art have seldom been produced unaided. Behind them has been, more often than not, a patron who knew exactly what he wanted and where it was to go. In this sense we all have the chance to leave some monument in our name, some addition to the landscape, some gateway, fountain or well. It is good, surely, to leave that much of oneself behind.

CHAPTER NINE

Teenology

Teenology is the study and discussion of the values, the conventions, the clothes, the music, the dancing, the art, the drinks and the drugs which are characteristic of the teen-age world. Fashions alter so quickly that any definition of what teen-agers appreciate would be out of date before this book could be published. If there is a continuity of ideas, however, it would lie in the rejection of the European tradition and the preference for the emotions and noises which originate in Africa.

The background to this choice is historically interesting but its immediate convenience lies in the fact that adult supervision is thus avoided. To dance the Minuet or the Gay Gordons means going to older people to ask how it is done. To play the music of Mozart means learning first how classical music is played. No such instruction is needed by the devotee of African rhythm, nor could his parents assist him with advice. This helps to create and define the teen-age environment from which the older generation is excluded. There are things, it is implied, which the elderly can hardly be expected to understand. Some teen-agers have thus come to live in a world of their own.

Various causes can be found for this state of affairs, but the first in importance is clearly the lack of parental authority in the home. This depended, a century ago, upon the convention of the husband being master in his own house. The wife gave him a formal obedience, realizing that upon this depended her authority in turn over the children. She was likely to see much more of them and her own efforts to maintain discipline might thus be weakened by familiarity. It was always her best plan, therefore, to fall back on the authority of an absent husband, saying "Your father has forbidden it," often with the inference that she herself would have been more indulgent. It was only by accepting her husband's sway that she could gain obedience from the young. The decision might be hers, but the unpopularity was his, the more easily borne in that he might not be there. To precepts about subordination, she thus added the potent force of example. Children and servants were in this way taught to know their place.

If parental authority would seem to have reached a peak in the Victorian age, it was essentially because the children had become so numerous. With a rather sudden reduction of infant mortality, the family might come to number twelve, fourteen, and even twenty. This turned the home into what was virtually a private school, with discipline required as never before. That children should never speak unless addressed may be desirable in any case, but when they come to number a dozen or so it becomes essential. Without the headmaster life had become impossible. So mother did everything to uphold father's prestige, using that in turn to protect herself. "I shall have to inform your father when he returns from the office." With these dreaded words she kept order, bringing tension to a climax with the announcement "I think I hear your father's foot upon the stairs!" She was not as terrified of him as she pretended to be but the pretense served a useful purpose. The children were petrified before the reproof had even begun and the result was a household in which there was relative peace and quiet. It could not probably have been ruled in any other way.

In the twentieth century children became fewer and the feminist revolt was the result. With discipline no longer the chief problem, the pattern of family life underwent a change. Granted a small number of children carefully spaced out, there might, it was thought, be time to reason with them. There might even be time to read books of child psychology. Father's word had no longer the authority of holy writ and even the Bible itself was relegated to a high shelf as quite unsuitable for the young. Why should women accept their subordinate role? Why indeed?

With some hesitation their claim to equality was conceded. The word "obey" was dropped from the marriage service or assumed, by mutual agreement, to mean something else. Among the intelligent there would henceforth be an easier relationship, a more casual comradeship and cooperation, with love to take the place of fear. Married women now retained their property and some of them even pursued separate careers; and most men welcomed the change, readily dropping their role of infallible tyrant in the home. The atmosphere henceforth would be one of informality and ease with problems brought into the open and difficulties fearlessly discussed. There is good reason for thinking that the husband contemporary with A. A. Milne was a more pleasant and kinder man than the husband who had been the contemporary of Charles Dickens. Family jokes had taken the place of family prayers. The Old Testament had been replaced by *Winnie the Pooh*.

What people were so slow to observe was that emancipation of the wife destroyed the parents' authority over the children. The mother did not exemplify the obedience upon which she still tried to insist. There was more room now for disagreement between the parents, enabling the child to appeal from one to the other, eventually ignoring both. In bringing the man down from his pedestal, the wife and mother deprived herself, in fact, of the means of discipline. To the question "Why can't we play with the hose nozzle?" she could no longer answer "Because father has forbidden it." She had now to reply "Because I say you mustn't." That she found difficult, and her instinct was to reason rather than command. The children must leave the hose nozzle alone because the neighbors might object, because the water might be wasted, because clothes might be soaked and because the children themselves might catch pneumonia and die. But in matters of discipline she who argues is lost. All she finally exacts is a feeble undertaking that they will be careful, a promise instantly forgotten and broken. Worse than any of the immediate consequences is the children's realization that mother can always be lured into an argument and that father will do nothing even when he learns about the damage done. The tearful wife who finally asks, "Why don't you use your influence?" is appealing to an authority she has herself undermined. Finding herself in this weak position, she tells herself and others that the old kind of discipline will not do for the modern child. He is to be reasoned with, but not coerced. Forms of address have been weakened from the Victorian "Sir," to the later "Daddy," and from that to the first name or else "Poor Pop." The final conclusion is that the problem of discipline must be left to the school.

The school, however, has itself been weakened by the influence of John Dewey (1859-1952), who urged that authoritarian methods should be abandoned and that pupils should learn by experience. The resulting system of "progressive" education has since permeated the schools, allowing the progressively minded to rejoice in fifty years of enlightenment. The gloomy Gothic prison, with shabby battered desks and flyblown steel engravings of the Parthenon, has been replaced by brightly furnished and glass-sided classrooms with pastel-shade decor and televised uplift. About the final result, different opinions are possible. What is certain, however, is that the process takes a very long time. Education on these lines would seem to go on for years and years and then for years again. For upwards of fifteen years — rising toward a quarter, perhaps, of many a lifetime — the immature and adolescent are herded together in the gaily decorated corridors of the coeducational school.

This may seem to contrast happily with the older practice of throwing children into the adult world, apprentices at seven or cabin boys at ten. A century ago the young were always thus outnumbered by the fully grown, whether in the stable yard, the barracks or the forecastle. In the progressive school, by comparison, there are no adults to fear or imitate, for the teacher is paid (it is thought) to behave in a certain way and is to be regarded, therefore, as peculiar and apart. The young are left to create a world of their own.

If these endless years at school, cut off from adult society, provide the background to the teen-age problem, the foreground is certainly occupied by the means of transport. Given a motorcycle or car, some money and a fine weekend, the young can do what they please. Nor is it easy to deny them the use of a car, for this has become necessary to their and our way of life, not a convenience so much as a bare necessity without which they must be miserably marooned and morose. Their weekends and vacations come therefore to be spent not with their elders but with each other. In the teen-age world they remain until such time as they finally quit school or college and have, for the first time, to earn a living.

It must be admitted, in defense of the young, that the community from which they seek to remain apart is not particularly inspiring. The trouble is, moreover, that the dullness of this adult environment is something the parents may have achieved with blood, sweat and tears. Life for many a couple began in a slum where drug-peddling and prostitution were among the familiar types of livelihood, where violence was common and murder not unknown. By self-education and saving, by enterprise and overwork, they have gained a higher level in society. To them the suburban house with its double garage represents success of a kind which they had once thought barely possible. There is high romance for them in the name on the gate, in the grass on the lawn. All has been earned by planning and patience, by thrift and by toil. But what seems so wonderful to them is nothing to their children, who have never, perhaps, known anything else. All the children can see is a dull suburb where the highest drama is represented by a mild scandal or an epidemic of measles. "Nothing ever happens here!" they protest. The parents, on their side, can remember times when all too much would happen too often. To live an uneventful life has been their highest ambition, pursued even now with determination and effort. This is more, however, than they can easily explain. It becomes an accepted fact that older people are unadventurous and humdrum, that the young are naturally bored with the adult way of life and that to escape from it all is their inevitable aim.

If the suburban home lacks any magnetic attraction for the young, the world of business has, if anything, less. For the terms of entry to that club, formidable enough at the outset, are often raised successively as the symptoms of revolt appear. The price of admission to responsible office is sometimes, perhaps, a too slavish observance of the accepted rules. It may be coupled, moreover, with an unduly prolonged novitiate. We are often told that the accent today is on youth. But ours has been the age of Nehru, Macmillan and Mao Tse-tung, of Adenauer, Franco and de Gaulle. When the old cling to authority it is not merely the middle-aged who despair, but the young who refuse even to mount the first rung of the ladder. To be doomed to thirty years of subordination is discouragement enough, but the prospect of fifty years' frustration must bring all to a standstill.

If the old would remove themselves, on the other hand, the promotion of the middle-aged would give the opportunity to youth. Where the young are maddened by their impotence, it is no answer to summon a few of them (aged twenty) to join the Councils of the Wise and Good. The proper remedy is to pension all over sixty and so make room for those aged twenty-seven. With some likelihood of responsible office in seven years' time, the young will quickly gain maturity. While we may be influenced by the teaching to which we have been exposed, we are still more influenced by the years of frustration which plainly lie ahead. Nor does it serve any purpose to create positions of imagined authority. The Club's Junior Committee deceives nobody, least of all when the real committeemen are all impossibly old. The responsibility offered to the young may not have to be immediate, but it does have to be real.

Organizations like the Boy Scouts are admirable, no doubt,

in intention, but they are fatally weakened at the outset by the fact that they are planned by age for youth. The stronger organization is one in which the adult call to the young for help in a common purpose, as in manning the lifeboat or arranging the pageant. Thinking of the evils which may result from idleness and rejecting the remedies offered by the youth organization, the modern father will sometimes decide on a home-made plan to keep his children out of mischief. He will announce some project like the construction of a sailing dinghy. There is initial enthusiasm and the backyard is soon filled with the bustling activity which father wanted to see. Planks are sandpapered, sails are stitched and rigging is greased. The boys are no longer hanging around with their hands in their pockets. The daughter is lured away from the drugstore and mother is delighted that the family should be together. But the joint effort is eventually seen to be artificial. The dinghy when launched is no better and little cheaper than the dinghy they might have bought. A fiberglass hull would have been in some ways preferable. All father has done is to arrange an instructive pastime for himself and the children. Instead of leaving them to play with their friends he has asked them to play instead with him, not because he needed their help but because he wanted to keep them occupied. The unreality of the situation derives from the fact that father is a stockbroker, not a canal boatman. Were the craft essential to his business the project would command the children's respect. But the boat is a toy and essentially their toy, not his. They come to feel in the end, that the whole project is childish, a man's attempt to join in a nursery game; nor is it, of necessity, the game they would have chosen for themselves. Father has to finish the dinghy single-handed, realizing at the same time that the scheme has failed. It is true that he has himself kept out of mischief, but the boys are now as idle as before and his daughter is again to be found with the local undesirables. Is there, asks father, no other way?

The only final answer is to allow the young to grow up, with the prospect of an earlier chance to use what talents they have. Failing that, they recoil from society and decide to remain in the teen-age world forever. This is the origin of that movement which has arisen almost simultaneously in places as remote from each other as San Francisco, Berlin and Tokyo, Amsterdam, London and Paris. The character of the movement is continually changing, but it begins, invariably, with the urge to escape. The means of escape are, broadly, six, namely: sex, speed and sound, dreams, drink and drugs. Nearest to reality of these is sex, the partner in which is at least a real person. Partly sexual again is the motorcyclist's love of violence and speed, the sensation of dominance and power. But the sound of the roaring engine merges again with the African rhythms which are the modern substitute for music. The hypnotic throb of the percussion instruments can induce the sort of trance in which the real world becomes a shadow, in which the dream becomes the fact. While all this record-playing, moaning and whining is a sad commentary upon our schooling, it cannot be said to do much physical damage. The mischief begins when the retreat from reality has to be hastened by drink or, now as commonly, by drugs. Tobacco is the mildest of these, a mere sedative, but the trend is toward those which give a stronger sense of illusion.

To condemn the drug addict is easy. To deride the banner-bearing and bearded half-wits in some pitiful procession of protest is easier still. What is far more difficult is to

create an adult society to which the young will clamor for admission. A start can be made, however, in any family where the need for responsibility is recognized. The secret is for the parents to decide on a goal which is just beyond their reach, calling upon the children to assist them in achieving what would be otherwise impossible. A perfectly proper aim is to make money, perhaps in order to move to a better home. The acquisition or construction of a country cottage may be a sound move, more especially if a certain child were named from the start as heir to the property. The success of parental (or of any other) leadership must always depend upon having a goal which is seen to be desirable and which is almost — but never quite — impossible to achieve. The point at which children lose interest is when neither community nor family have any object beyond what is easily attainable or has been already attained. Whether the aim is idealistic or selfish is, from this point of view, immaterial. The point is that an effort is being made and that the children are invited — and, indeed, required — to take part in it. They are urged, in fact, to become adult.

To solve the problems of Teenology it is essential, then, to create a society in which the young have their part to play, not as a pressure group, not merely as pupils, but as junior members of the team. Among the loudest in condemnation of rebellious youth are old men at the head of organizations in which no one under sixty has ever had more than routine work to do. When sufficiently alarmed, these elderly autocrats will sometimes offer some sweeping concession to the very junior. What they refuse to do is resign! Failing that there is the situation which leads to revolt and to our final conclusion that the young are simply revolting. Such are our fears, however, for the institutions threatened that we seldom notice what damage is being done to the young themselves. For the shouting of slogans, whether derived from Malcolm X or Chairman Mao, is a sign of retarded development. Nor do the young emerge unscathed from a teen-age devoted to speed and noise, to dreams and drugs. Even if physically unharmed, the chance they have thrown away — the chance of reaching an intellectual maturity — is gone and is gone for good.

Osborn

CHAPTER TEN

Escape

WHETHER she has teen-age children or not, the housewife has her moments of frustration and despair; ended, normally, as soon as shared. There are, however, some periods of boredom and nausea which are not as easily brought to an end. The married man is not immune from these, and it is at least theoretically possible that he might succumb at the same time as his wife.

It is similarly possible, but extremely unlikely, that two candles should go out at the same moment. Granted the improbability of this, we can suppose that the collapse of one partner would act as a stimulus to the other. Ruling out, for the moment, the case in which both have been poisoned by the same shellfish, we may assume that one of the two will be reasonably effective and cheerful at any given time. The other, less fortunate, will complain perhaps that everything is so expensive, that her daughters have become impossible, that the house is damp and that her best friends have all left the vicinity. If only she could escape from it all! In point of fact her need is to escape from herself. This can be done in various ways, the most obvious of which is to get sick. This depends for its effect, however, on someone else in the house remaining sympathetic, attentive and well.

That the patient is the accomplice of the disease is usually shown by the timing of its onset. One must presume that the germ is there all along and that the victim lowers her subconscious guard at a moment when it suits her to be ill. It is impossible for some people to arrange a holiday in any other way. At the given moment, when the guests have left or when the children have gone back to school, the temperature rises, the pain develops, the weakness becomes apparent and the illness takes charge.

It is not — let us be clear about this — a case of malingering. The complaint is not imaginary, the symptoms are real, the indisposition will run its course and the aftereffects will follow a textbook pattern. It could not happen, nevertheless, without the patient's subconscious consent, nor did it happen when circumstances would have made it impossibly inconvenient. The need for a rest may partly account for the illness, but there also enters into it the need to escape.

For the period spent in bed the patient avoids not only the daily routine but her workaday personality. She assumes a different character; that, for example, of a martyr whose courage is an inspiration to everyone else. Hating to be a burden to her friends, she struggles on almost to the end. Only afterward do people realize how she must have suffered. Pale and feeble as she may be, she has always a thought for others. Saintliest of the saintly, she is also the bravest of the brave.

In illness as in war, heroism is not enough in itself. To be effective it requires a public. There must be someone to see and sympathize, someone to notice how the twinge of pain is instantly replaced by a wan smile of resignation. A more numerous public — nurses, physicians and relatives — would of course be preferable; but one is the minimum, without which the whole thing becomes pointless. That one will be the husband or wife as the case may be and nothing strains a marriage more than a failure to play this part as it should be played.

When the wife says, "I have a splitting headache," the good husband should register anxiety by admitting that she looks unwell.

"You poor darling! You are pale too, come to think of it. I doubt if your pulse is normal. Take two aspirins now while I fetch a cold compress. Then I'll phone the club and tell them that you won't be able to attend this afternoon's committee session."

How unfeeling, by comparison, is the husband who dismisses her complaints as imaginary. "Funny," he says, "because you *look* all right. Maybe it's a hangover from last night's party. See you after the committee meeting!"

This is an example of inhuman brutality, the man simply refusing to see that his wife is on the danger list. It is shocking to think that such men exist, monsters (to coin a phrase) in human form; sadists who care nothing for the misery which others have to endure but who are themselves insufferable when they have so much as a cold in the head.

Still worse than anything so far described is the conduct of one who matches one complaint with another. It is of the essence of the marital relationship that only one can be ill at a given time. The one who first complains must be deemed to have priority, the other to remain well until a fictitious traffic light turns green. To cross against the red light is still, however, possible and the crime may be committed with some such dialogue as this:

"Oh, Tom, I feel weak and giddy as if I might faint at any moment."

"That's just how I feel, Mabel. I wonder if brandy would do any good?"

"I feel sick too."

"Same here. I'll bet it was that crab cocktail. It tasted queer at the time."

"It's my heart — the beat is irregular."

"I often have that feeling. It comes from indigestion."

"I don't know how to get through the day. God knows I've struggled to keep going but this pain in the chest is too much for me."

"So *you* have that too? I've been wondering whether I have thrombosis."

"I simply have to lie down."

"Just what I mean to do. But will you phone the doctor first?"

Now the situation implied by this conversation is plainly impossible. Husband and wife cannot be ill at the same time. Tom's conduct is deplorable because Mabel announced her illness first. When she began, "I feel weak and giddy . . ." it was *his* cue to reply, "Come and lie down on the sofa while I make you a cup of tea." Ignoring his obvious duty, however, he has to babble about his own imagined symptoms. On these lines he will end by driving the poor girl out of her mind. To demand sympathy from a woman who needs it herself is no more nor less than mental cruelty, and husbands have been divorced for less. So the situation in this imagined case is extremely serious and we may fairly ask whether the marriage is likely to survive. Its prospects are poor, we must conclude, while the husband refuses to wait his turn. There is a time for everything and no husband should be ill until his wife has recovered.

As a means of escape, fiction is alternative to illness and ancillary to convalescence. Fiction can be provided in the form of television, radio, novel, motion picture or play. The

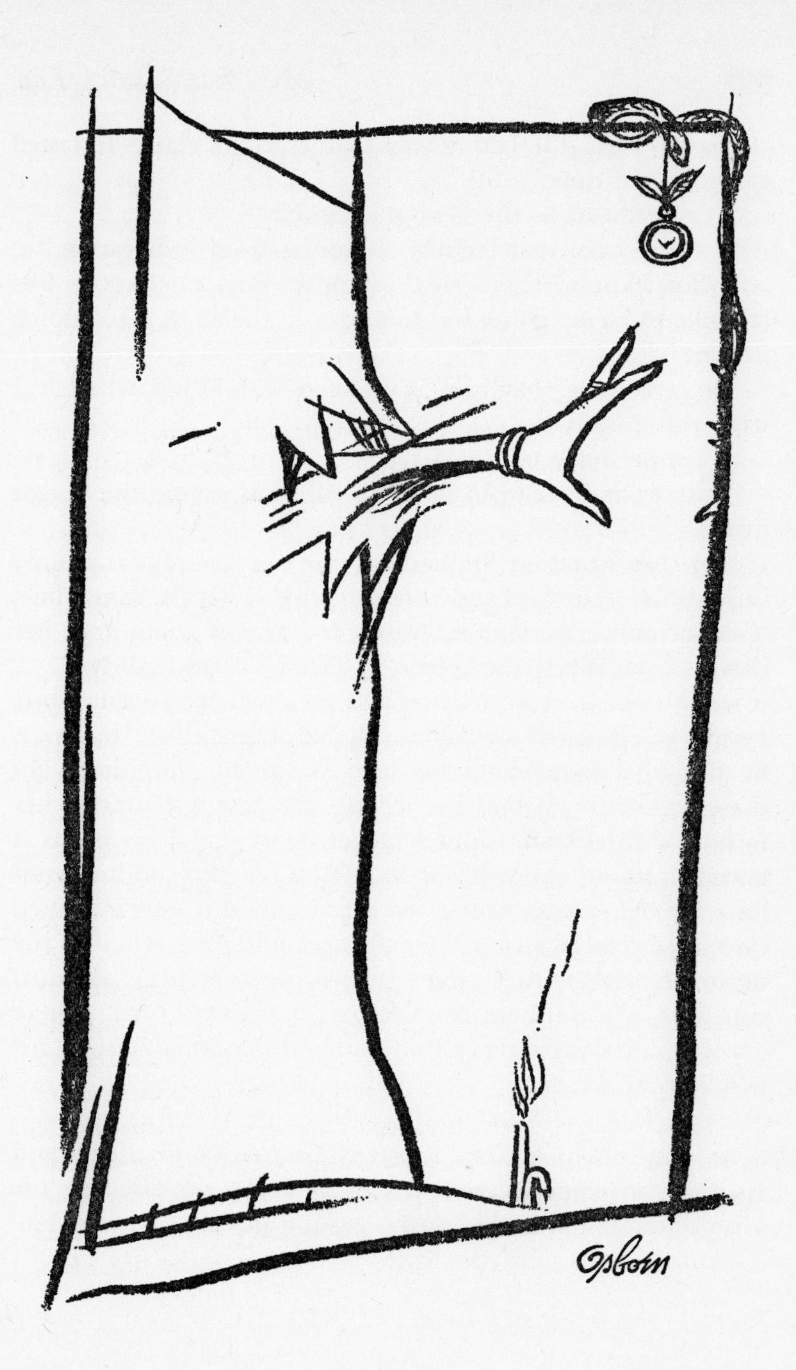

object is to shut out one's real environment and live, for a time, in an imaginary world. Some children spend most of their time in daydreams, needing little stimulus from television or the printed page. For the television addicts of the twentieth century, less and less is left to the imagination, and whereas Shakespeare told his audience to picture the battlefield for themselves, the modern producer has to show us the bloodshed in Technicolor.

This sort of entertainment alternates, it is true, with discussion and comment on actual events. The eventual result is to confound fact with fiction, the producer being even more confused than the audience. Confusion between real and simulated drama is nearly always to the advantage of the latter, statesmen of the studio being infinitely more statesmanlike than the politicians for whom we are invited to vote. A confusion of ideas thus leads us to conclude that the film star or popular singer is a person whose views should be invited on the problems of the day. Brought before the camera, the great actor-manager is asked his opinion on foreign policy or the balance of trade. He has no views. Why should he? He has devoted his whole life to representing the characters of other people, fictitious or real, and to dramatizing their points of view. He could never have succeeded as a player had he been stuffed with opinions of his own.

But television viewers are slow to realize that administrative and acting abilities are not merely different but opposite. As the line between fiction and reality becomes blurred, radio and the television screen offer a dwindling means of escape from reality. The illusion of the story is continually interrupted, not merely by advertising but by the producer's inability to decide what he is trying to do. *Entertainment* he may freely offer — the operatic song, the comedian's patter — but this is not, of course, an escape from life. It is merely a noise which we have come to accept as the background to other activities. As for the well-documented television series which deals with the current scene, that has least escape value of all, being usually more sordid than life itself.

As a restful escape from the world the novel is probably still supreme. It is chosen by the individual, not imposed by a producer's idea of what the average taste should demand. More than that, it is chosen to suit a particular situation or mood; a thriller for the train journey, a romance for the air passage, a cloak-and-dagger for the bedside and something soporific for the living room sofa.

As compared with the television play, the novel is much longer, giving the author time to build up the background to his story. The average reader is willing to accept the improbable but needs time to learn what the conventions are to be. The late Mr. Ernest Bramah placed all his stories in the context of a conventionally willow-pattern China of an undefined but remote dynasty, all dialogue being ceremonious, long-winded and infinitely polite. This is an atmosphere which takes time to establish, and something of the same approach is required in a story about King Arthur and Merlin. Illusion is acceptable but we need to know what the illusion is to be.

Most successful in this way is the three-volume Victorian novel, in which the reader can really lose herself, as for example in Trollope's *Barchester Towers*. A work of that length allows the addict to enter fully into the story, identifying with one of the characters and becoming involved in many of the situations. To put the book down, as for example to answer the telephone, causes a mental shock, proof in itself that the escape from real life has been complete.

As against that, the sort of detective story which poses a problem can be read only once and is spoiled even by a preknowledge of who the criminal will turn out to be. But the big novels of the nineteenth century do not depend upon a surprise finish but upon their capacity for holding our attention even on a second or third reading. Finding ourselves in another society, we have escaped for the time from the environment in which we ordinarily live. It may be that the world of fiction is more attractive than the world of truth, but that is less significant than the fact that it is different. For the time of the reading we have been emphatically away from home.

Can a motion picture serve the same purpose as a novel? The truth would seem to be that its effect is short-lived. While our attention can be captured more quickly by tricks with the camera, our total involvement is less. For one thing, attendance at the cinema is, to some extent, a social art. We form part of an audience and we remain aware of the audience reaction. We may feel at one moment that we are charging with General Custer or fighting the Zulus at Rorkes Drift, but we are jerked back to the present when a child says "Ooooh!" in the row behind. Nor are we likely to have entered the motion picture theater alone in the first place. The experience is thus shared with husband or daughter, with someone who belongs to our everyday life, with someone who may even resent our enthusiasm being excessive. "You think Elizabeth Taylor *beautiful?*" asks the wife pointedly, and the husband is careful to explain that girls can be attractive *in different ways* (if you see what I mean), that Miss Taylor has her public but that his own purely personal preference is for blondes aged about thirty-seven. The cinema-goer may thus have to watch his step, conscious that he or she is not alone.

Apart from that, the story is too often overshadowed by the

players and the acting over-dramatized beyond the limits of the credible. One objection, among several, to the publicity buildup of the cinema star is that we are aware all along who the chief performer is. The more we admire Rex Harrison as an actor, the less do we accept him as Julius Caesar or Professor Higgins. In a dozen ways the motion picture may be inspiring and instructive but it rarely transports us for long into a different place and time. We are too conscious of the casting and the cutting, too interested to distinguish between sequences shot on location or in the studio. We may be enthralled but we are seldom deceived.

Where our object is to escape from our humdrum existence, the theater has less to offer than the films. For theater-going is a still more social act, allowing us to greet our friends in the interval and discuss with them the merits of the cast. If we no longer dress for the occasion as we used to do, we are still very consciously part of an audience, playing a part, therefore, in the success or failure of the show. While we are thus involved in the performance we are only mildly lost in the story. Theater-goers remain themselves — except when very young — being anxious to look distinguished and well-dressed or eager to show that they have guessed how the play will end. Where the cast is repertory or amateur we are still more critical, noting that Eric is less effective than he was in an older part or registering surprise that Margaret can act as well as she does. The people who gain most from the amateur stage are, of course, the players themselves. For the keenest of them the part is a splendid escape from life. This is a fact we should bear in mind even if our own activity should go no further than charades. There is admittedly something daunting in the amount of work which must go into an amateur play. It is strange, therefore, that so few people attempt an easier alternative with marionettes. The puppet theater, which can obviate the need to learn a part, is not inferior in giving us access to another world. Strutting the boards by deputy, we can play the part of highwayman or shepherdess, sheriff or queen. In roles such as these the characters of executive and housewife can be momentarily but happily lost.

The last and most obvious way of escape is offered by the weekend and the summer holidays. These afford, to begin with, a change of surroundings. People who live in the plain can go to the mountains and people who live in the forest can go to the sea. More than that, there can be a change of occupation, the banker becoming a fisherman and the harassed mother becoming a lady of leisure. Where the children come too there is, it is true, an element of continuity, holiday parents having to be parents still. There can, however, be a different atmosphere and a change at least of emphasis.

Where the difficulty lies is in the differing tastes of men and women. Given the opportunity of a long weekend, father begins to dream of the lakeside camp or the mountain chalet. Mother is more likely to dream of a luxury suite in the Grand Hotel. The difference between them arises from the fact that whereas every girl grows into a woman the average boy will always remain (to some extent) a boy. The girl who plays with a doll is thus rehearsing what her role in life is actually to be. When she cares for her pony, her maternal instincts are already involved, her emotional needs already met. The boy, by contrast, prepares for a career he is unlikely to follow. He sees himself as backwoodsman or cowboy, as secret agent or submarine commander. In a very few instances the dream becomes reality, as when a model enthusiast becomes an engineer. But whoever heard of boys playing a game based on market analysis or automobile insurance? In the majority of cases, the would-be Lone Ranger ends as a public accountant.

The general tendency is thus for men to be eternally dissatisfied, looking back to the life of adventure which has been denied them. Instead of playing with stockades and rifles, wild animals and outlaws, they are forced to play merely with pieces of paper. Inside each executive is an exasperated man of action, longing for the opportunities which have been denied him. We may question, if we will, whether Walter Mitty would respond too readily to the actual emergency if it came, but there can be no doubt at all concerning his inner frustration. It reveals itself in his plans for the weekend away from home. He begins at once to see himself as the husky frontiersman, the builder of the log cabin, the fisherman and game-hunter, expert with the knife and ax. Common sense may substitute a cabin cruiser for the camp in the wilds, but he then sees himself as an old salt who has been around the Horn before the mast. The daydream will vary from day to day, but it will always involve dealing practically with things instead of documents. Once in his element he is not to be recognized as the man his colleagues know at the office Given a storm at sea his family will see him, for the first time, as the man he really is.

Mother's outlook is totally different. Her dreams as a schoolgirl were admittedly much nearer to the life she actually lives, but this differs nevertheless from her more hopeful anticipations. Her favorite romance involved a girl who fell in love with a poor boy, only to discover (on their honeymoon) that he is really a millionaire. She had loved him, you see, *for himself alone* and the fact that he stood to inherit the Dukedom came as a tremendous shock. Surviving this cruel deception, she then begins to realize that there might be some minor advantages in her position; her personal maid being the first and the Chef — a genius in his way — being the second. This dream admitted of variations, but its general purport was to leave her with a town and country house, plenty of servants and an unlimited dress allowance.

That was the schoolgirl vision but her life has been significantly different. Harry is the best husband in the world, mind you, and his salary, since the last raise, has been almost adequate. He is far, however, from being a millionaire in disguise, his actual income being rather less than she had supposed it to be when their engagement was announced. Domestic help is not among the luxuries they can afford, but a new dress might be picked up on sale after Christmas. With careful economy she has achieved a level of reasonable comfort; but luxury has not so far come her way.

For Mother, so situated, the camping holiday has few attractions. Her role in the cabin cruiser or trailer will be to cook the meals while father is caulking the deck or pitching the tent. Her dreams as a schoolgirl had never involved a life under canvas, and the heroine's part in western films is always rather marginal to the story. If not actually captured by the enemy (as might be thought normal), the most the heroine can do is to reload the hero's rifle and have a meal ready when the last redskin has bitten the dust.

But this role merely brings her back to the kitchen sink, the only difference being that the weekend kitchen is badly equipped. The galley stove is a poor substitute for the electric one and there is an eternal likelihood that something will have been forgotten — the bottle opener, for instance, or the butter. 'But I thought *you* had packed it," they tell each other, and father tries to think what Buffalo Bill or Sir Francis Chichester would have done in a similar crisis.

The basic trouble, however, is that father's adventure is merely mother's inconvenience. Attempts to shoot the neck off the bottle are, to her, merely tiresome and childish. If that is to set the tone of the vacation she would rather be at home with the saucepans where she can find them and the shops close at hand. As compared with the average man, a woman is incurably and unforgivably adult.

Mother's dream holiday begins when her expensive car drives up to the door of the Hotel Stupendous. Escorted by her husband, looking more distinguished than he does in actual life, she is bowed into the building. While servants handle her pigskin luggage, she notices a group of celebrities gathered round the lobby fireplace. Center of attraction is the Princess of Ruritania who suddenly looks round and sees who the new arrival is. "Belinda *darling!*" she exclaims and Mother is brought at once into the circle, which comprises the Duke of Midlothian, Olga Stormoff, Senator Stetson, the Countess Gleeson and the Carolingian Ambassador. She finds, to her faint surprise, that she knows them all intimately and that they treat her husband (now three inches taller) with a certain deference. The hotel manager informs her that she is to have the Imperial Suite with the rather unique view over the lake. "That explains," says the Princess, in mock disgust, "why I was not allowed to have it!"

It is soon apparent that they are not to dine at the hotel because the Duke insists upon their all having potluck with him at the Schloss Blankenburg-Staritz, which he has borrowed for the season from his old friend the Freiherr von Sauerkraut. "Nothing very grand," he admits, "but the castle is floodlit and we shall have the bagpipes." This plan is accepted by all as a basically sound idea.

At this point in the dream another car draws up at the hotel entrance. Mother recognizes it as the convertible driven by her rival for the chairmanship of the Parent-Teacher Association, the intolerable Mrs. Sandra Sopping. The convertible has turned itself into an earlier model before colliding with the gatepost, but Sandra and her dim little husband have cleverly repaired the fender themselves, he using a hammer and she a tin of nearly-matching varnish paint from Woolworth's. This recent accident would seem to have aged her somewhat and Cedric's suit looks more ill-fitting than usual.

The conversation dies away as they shuffle, carrying their luggage, toward the reception desk. The general manager has vanished and the room clerk is a beetle-browed man of forbidding appearance. Under the hostile stare of the group by the fireplace, the Soppings mutter something about having made a reservation by telephone. With great deliberation the clerk opens the ledger and runs his finger down the page.

"What name did you say?"

"Cedric Sopping."

"Sopping . . . *Sopping* . . . I have no entry under that name. On what date did you telephone?"

"On the 13th."

"The day before yesterday? We should hardly be able to accommodate you at such short notice as that. The hotel is full and our rooms are all booked years in advance."

"But you accepted the reservation."

"I'm sorry, sir, we have no trace of it."

"This is disgraceful!"

"Perhaps there has been some mistake. What number did you call?"

"I made a note of it, as it happens, in my diary . . . Yes, here it is . . . Hotel Stupendous, Nitwitz 258634."

"Our number, sir, is St. Moritz 6000."

"At what hotel, then, did I make the booking?"

At this point Sandra intervenes with some asperity, asking him how the clerk can possibly know. But she is wrong again, for the clerk has a sudden inspiration. Reaching for the telephone directory, he glances through the section under I.

"The number you called would seem to be that of the Hotel Imbecilia."

"And where," asks Sandra, "is that?"

The bored clerk flips the pages of the *Guide Michelin* and reads the relevant extract in a splendidly audible voice:

"*Imbecilia,* 423 Schmellengasse, Nitwitsenberg (Pop. 297,000), Grade 9, Bedrooms 5, no both, no meals, no garage, closed on Sunday."

"Oh, God!" says Sandra. "It's Friday and all the other hotels will be full."

"I agree, Madam, that this is probably the case."

"How far away is this dump?"

"About two hundred and eighty miles."

"We shall need some more gas even to make it!"

"That reminds me, dear," says the wretched Cedric, "that I seem to have left my wallet at home. . . ."

"But you have a credit card??"

"That is in the wallet. . . . I wondered whether *you* had any money with you?"

"Why should I? And what do we do now?"

"Well, I'm sure that this hotel would cash a check?" The clerk at the reception desk begins to look more forbidding than ever. The tone of his voice when he replies is about ten degrees colder than it was when they first arrived.

"I'll ask the assistant manager, sir. May I assume, however, that you have some means of identification, or are known to some guest who is staying here?"

Cedric's documents are, of course, in the missing wallet, but Sandra at this moment catches sight of Mother, and almost sobs with relief. Moving quickly in that direction, she trips over the tiger-skin rug and is promptly bitten in the ankle. Recovering herself with an effort, Sandra approaches the group by the fireplace, eyed by all with frank disgust.

"Marvelous to see you, dear!" she gibbers. "Do please tell the receptionist that we are known to you as your neighbors in Whatsitville!"

There is a deathly hush while Mother studies Sandra's appearance, looking her over carefully from head to foot. When she speaks, however, it is not to Sandra but to the clerk at the desk.

"I never saw the woman before in my life!"

Osborn

CHAPTER ELEVEN

Travel

As we have seen, the weekend and summer holidays are usually, not always, the opportunity to escape. They may give Father his chance, on occasion, to play his favorite role as pioneer or sea dog. They may sometimes allow Mother to play at being a great lady, with money no object and time to spare. Where both play fair, the roles will alternate, the wife putting up with the discomfort of the sailing boat, the husband enduring the boredom of the hotel lounge. While the children are young the boat will be more often in use, but as they grow older the balance may tip the other way.

In the meanwhile, however, and increasingly, both husband and wife must consider the question of travel; not merely to a ski resort but to somewhere more exotic. Their position, after all, requires that they should have some knowledge of the world. Their friends, moreover, are always talking about Morocco, Minorca and Marrakesh, about Brunei, Brasília and Bâle. Among the widely traveled they feel inferior, reduced to muttered explanations as to why they go no further afield. The time for adventure would seem to have come, and travel literature is heaped on the coffee table as they compare the merits of Portugal, Mozambique, Scotland, and Syria, Paraguay, Uruguay, Norway and Spain. The choice will be impossible, however, if they fail to decide in advance what exactly they are trying to achieve.

If we exclude travel undertaken for the prosaic purposes of diplomacy, business or war, the possible objects of going abroad are, broadly speaking, three. One can, to begin with, avoid all or part of the winter by going to some place where the climate is different. The chief advantage of travel for this purpose is a negative one, derived mainly from subsequent conversation, as thus:

George:	I don't suppose the winter here is very severe?
Olive:	You'd be surprised! We had two feet of snow last January with cars abandoned outside the supermarket. For two days we couldn't even leave the house.
Sarah:	Of course, we all said it was exceptional and I suppose it was. That's why we were unprepared, with no snowplows or anything. The children all loved it!
George:	How long did it last?
Olive:	There were two days when the children could not get to school — then there was the weekend. By Tuesday the snow had gone.
George:	What about you, Brian? You are very silent on this subject. I picture you digging the ambulance out of the snowdrift.
Brian (*modestly*):	I'm afraid not, George. I wasn't here. I spent January where I usually spend it — at my place in the Bahamas.

There is, of course, an art in saying this with the maximum effect. The remark must be delayed, for one thing, until the last possible moment. It must be uttered without a trace of too obvious satisfaction, but it must, at the same time, con-

vey just a hint of reproof. Where, for heaven's sake, did they *think* he would be in January? Wouldn't one be correct in assuming that everyone who matters will be in the West Indies at that time of year? This must be a fact, surely, of common knowledge? The fashionable restaurants in London and New York are empty then, and the waiters show their contempt for the few clients who may appear. Brian's words must imply all this and much besides and should reduce the table to an uneasy silence. A moment later everyone begins to talk brightly about something else; treating Brian, however, with a new respect. For Brian, let us face it, has scored.

Granted that absence can thus convey a sense of prestige, the trick of winter avoidance is still a negative achievement. The palm-fringed beach can be extremely dull, and what satisfaction its visitors gain is chiefly from not being somewhere else. This is even true of the winter cruise, which suffers still further from being purposeless. There is nothing to do but eat to excess, play deck games, swim and read, gamble and drink, dance and sleep. The entertainment offered would be perfectly adequate for young people aged eighteen to twenty-five, who would mix all these activities with flirtation and romance. But few of the young can afford to be there, those with the money and leisure being mostly over sixty. And even these, hardworking perhaps until recently, are haunted with a sense of guilt. Comparing themselves with the ship's officers and crew, they feel useless, extravagant, idle and dull. To this guilt complex they react with childish jokes and paper hats, being pitied the more by men who have work to do.

Entirely different is the atmosphere on board a ship that is bound for a sensible destination, its passengers still with a living to earn. The same games may be played but with a different purpose. Keeping fit, considered as an object, invites the question "For what?" and there are travelers whose reply can be emphatic and prompt. On a cruise ship the passengers must answer, lamely, "In order to overeat."

Better than any cruise now offered would be the Executive Conference Afloat, alternating with the Short University Course at sea. The first could combine lectures and seminars on Organization and Method with physical training, volleyball and the sauna bath. The second would offer courses in (say) Spanish, Navigation, Oceanography and Art, all to tie in with the trips ashore. On these more purposeful voyages the deck hands, stewards and waitresses might well be students working their passage and benefiting at the same time from some of the lectures.

All this has been done on a small scale, but shipowners have been slow, in general, to see that there might be a "permissive" element in the holiday; a positive gain that justifies the expense. With the mental stimulus there should also be offered a health routine. For the price of the ticket the passenger might thus have a medical examination, a special diet, a program of exercise and a guaranteed loss of weight by the end of the voyage. To travel hopefully is proverbially better than to arrive, which may be true. Hopefulness presupposes an object, however, and it is this which the shipowners fail, normally, to provide. Our absence for the winter may allow us to score over people who cannot afford it, but a more positive aim would do more for our own morale. A merely negative pleasure is, surely, not enough.

The second possible object of travel is to gain by boasting of where you have been. The mere process of travel is apt to be disappointing. If the tour is inclusive and highly organized the tourist finds that she must do as she is told. In spirit

Osborn

back at the Sunday school picnic she finds herself behaving in a childish way, putting her tongue out toward the guide's back or even flicking bread about at meals. Should the tour be unorganized, the drawbacks will include mendicants and customs officials, currency difficulties and pilfered luggage, mosquitoes and dysentery, sunburn and sweat. The tourist has also the sensation of being himself an object of curiosity, cheated and laughed at, pitied and despised. Wearing the correct uniform, the seasoned traveler disperses the beggars with a few rude words in the right dialect, boards the car that has been sent to meet him and relaxes presently on the club veranda. The tourist wears, by custom, his incongruous Bermuda shorts, dons some gaily ribboned straw hat, slings his camera about him and steps into a purgatory which is even worse for his wife. The camera is his badge of infamy, his certificate of third-class citizenship. It indicates that his aim is less to see anything than to boast about his travels afterward. He cannot enjoy but he wants to record.

Beyond all the present humiliation and discomfort, the tourist looks forward to the evening next fall when his captive audience is collected in the living room after dinner. The most effective use of the slide projector depends upon a husband-and-wife team, thus:

Host: This is Hong Kong at sunset with the lights just coming on. The junks and sampans you can see in the foreground have not changed for centuries. Thousands of people live in them, having no other home.

Hostess: Forgive me, dear, but I think that is actually Penang.

Host: But surely that is the Peak in the background, where the Tycoons live?

Hostess: You mean Baboons, dear. That is Penang Hill, reached by that cable car.

Host: Look, darling, I remember taking this picture near the Star Ferry, and you can see for yourself that the boats are all Chinese.

Hostess: Yes, my love, but the boats at Penang are Chinese, too. I actually took this picture myself. What's more, the figure on the left is *you.*

Host: Oh, rubbish! I never wore a hat like that.

Hostess: You are looking at the wrong figure, dearest. That is a Trishaw coolie. You are on *his* left again.

Host: I hate to contradict you, dear, but that man has a camera slung on his shoulder. How could *he* have had the camera if *you* were using it?

Hostess: I took it with *my* camera, darling!

Host: But your camera was stolen at Singapore. You didn't have it by the time we reached Hong Kong.

Hostess: I realize that, sweetheart, but I still had the camera at *Penang* — where this picture was taken — by *me.*

Host: Well, folks, we are not going to convince each other, so I'll go on to the next slide. It shows a yacht on a dead calm sea with the sails reflected in the water. I'm rather proud of this camera study.

Hostess: It's upside down.

Host: You mean the reflection is really the yacht?

Hostess: Yes. Try it the other way and you'll see.

Host: (*fumbling, twice putting it in sideways*) My goodness. I believe you're right, dear; not that it makes much difference . . . Anyway, this is a yacht in Singapore Harbor.

Hostess: It was actually in Kobe.

Host: *She* was at Kobe, you mean . . .

To the writhing audience it doesn't matter what any of the slides represent or which way up they are shown. All that concerns them is the length of time they must spend watch-

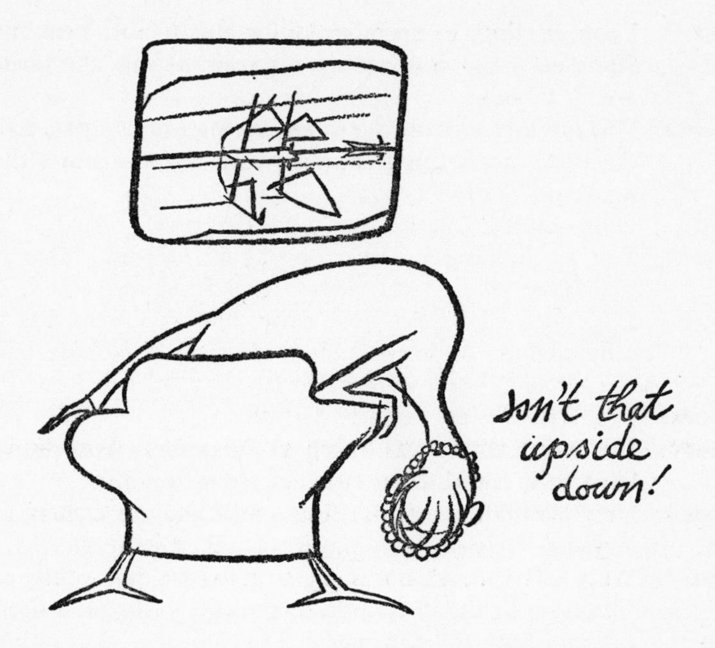

ing them. If each slide is going to take a minute and a half (the present average) and there are two thousand of them, covering the whole globe, they are going to be there for over two days. Their appearance of rapt attention is due to the calculation each is doing in his head and any hint of dejection is due to the answer he has reached.

Marginally worse is the travelogue presented in motion. While the basic idea may be the same, the technical performance is at a lower standard. Comparatively harmless as a memento of our children playing with the dog, or baby's first day on the beach, the motion picture becomes deadly as a record of travel. This is because the cameraman has usually failed to master the first principle of his art: that the object should be moving and the camera (usually) still. Impressed by the Taj Mahal or the Albert Memorial, the eager tourist waves the camera round it so as to ensure that no detail should escape. The picture which results from this headlong pursuit of the static has often made children actually sick.

The fact is that the Parthenon (or whatever the monument may be) is an unsuitable subject for motion pictures. Ideal, by contrast, is the finish of a horse race or the climax of a boxing match. But these are not the scenes which the tourist wants to record. Her anxiety is merely to prove that she has seen the Pyramids, the Capitol and the Eiffel Tower. She makes this point with a whirring camera, interspersing the architecture with candid shots of her sister-in-law.

The main objection to this strategy is that the camera addict is not really interested in the place she is visiting. If genuinely in love with Venice, she would have left her camera at the hotel and wandered, spellbound, round the Ca' d'Oro. The real lover of Rothenburg or La Rochelle is not so eager to share her pleasure with everyone else. She knows, to begin with, that the experience cannot be shared; that Venice is not a place to be photographed but a life to be lived. She knows, further, that the magic of the scene is only partly visual, that the Alpine pass includes the sound of the bells and the scent of the wildflowers. She knows, finally, that each lover of the open road must find a Carinthia of her own and will not be content with any other.

There is, however, a third object of travel, and that is to gain some real knowledge of the world. This means to have been everywhere and to know *some* foreign countries well. Such a knowledge is fully possessed only by those who traveled when young and poor. To decide in middle age that

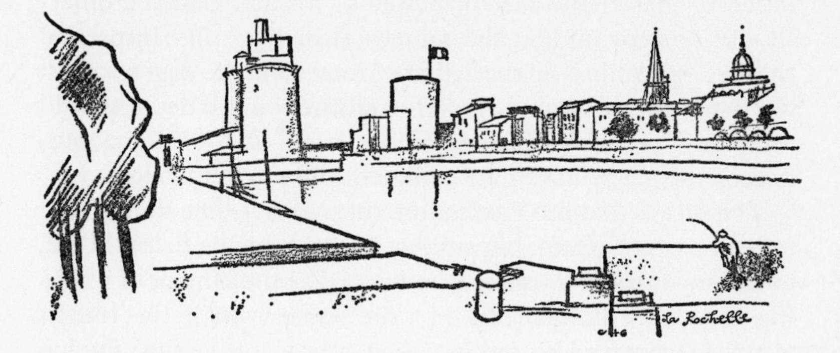

travel would broaden your mind is praiseworthy but no substitute for the travel you missed in youth. The France or Austria you see from the best hotel is quite different from that seen by the almost penniless boy with a knapsack, and one ought to know it from either point of view.

To the young the foreign land is a place of wonder and adventure, seen in a golden haze and vibrant with the possibilities of romance. In later years we are apt to make some comments upon the plumbing and the cover charge, the discomfort of the bedding and the noise made in emptying the garbage cans. Our more critical attitude does not make our later travel useless, but it does suggest that we should go, when more elderly, with a definite purpose. Ideally, we should have some specialist interest in certain aspects of a single country, or even in one aspect of a single town. While the process of self-education should begin with a general survey, wide reading followed by a brief visit perhaps to every continent, it should culminate in something like research. To have made oneself an authority on even the smallest corner of the most obscure subject is a great satisfaction in itself. It throws light, moreover, on every other field of knowledge. While one may have only a passing acquaintance with the results of current research, one knows, henceforth, how the trick is done.

It was once the tradition in Britain that a gentleman's education should begin at the grammar school and should involve a grounding in Latin and mathematics. It should be continued at the university where he did not necessarily graduate but where he was at least brought into contact with learning. With some idea of theology and philosophy, and knowing by now how to ride and fence, the young gentleman was next entered at one of the Inns of Court. Without being actually called to the Bar, he gained some knowledge of law and city life, often learning, incidentally, to play some musical instrument.

The time had now come for the Grand Tour, a leisurely progress through France, Austria and Italy. The object of this exercise, lasting for a year or two, was to gain some facility in languages and inspect, at the same time, the ruins of antiquity. Armed with a sheaf of introductions the young man was to be presented to the several monarchs and their advisers. No longer wholly ignorant of diplomacy, he completed his education by serving as a volunteer in whatever campaign might be suitable, most probably in the Netherlands. For some months at least he would take part in the current siege, living under canvas and coming under fire. A sortie by the garrison might lead to a skirmish, a clash of swords and perhaps even a superficial wound. With honor more than satisfied, the young gentleman could return home as a man of the world, as a man fit for public office.

To be a man or woman of the world, in this sense, is a very

proper ambition. Our international relationships would be vastly improved were we to elect no politician who was not so qualified. But there is a danger in the process of which we need to be aware. People who travel together are apt to quarrel. The speed of flight, the alterations of the clock, the currency regulations and the difficulties over language impose, between them, a growing tension. This is felt, however, unequally as between the husband and wife, or even between two friends who may travel together. One of them is the more relaxed, telling the other to stop worrying.

But this attitude, given emphasis by a tendency to read the newspaper while the other is packing, will make the tension worse. It is through this sort of overconfidence that things are left behind — things which might include a vaccination certificate or rail ticket. The likelihood of this — and it actually happened, on that visit to Amsterdam — makes the other one more inclined to fuss. The reaction to this is a refusal to get up in time, which in turn prevents the other even going to sleep. The friction which results is not specifically the fault of either, for each has driven the other to an extreme and either, in opposite circumstances, might have played the contrary part.

Where such a clash of temperaments takes place the scene at the airport might be dramatized as follows:

Sheila:	I'll get the papers and aspirins too.
Frederick:	You'll miss the plane, I keep telling you.
Sheila:	I need some eau de cologne and scent.
Frederick:	But what would you say if the dashed plane went?
Sheila:	I want some coffee. I'll phone my aunt.
Frederick:	I'll see to the tickets. I really can't stand more of your wanting this and that.
Sheila:	I've just remembered, I need a hat!

Frederick: Passport, currency, baggage check . . .
Sheila: I look — Oh, God — a perfect wreck!
Frederick: I'd best insure, and check the time.
Sheila: What I want is a gin-and-lime.
(*The flight is called.*)
Sheila: I like to sit right in the tail.
Frederick: The forward seats are always best.
Sheila: In case the engines all should fail.
Frederick: You've put it, have you, to the test?
Sheila: I'll want to read. You'll want to sleep.
Frederick: You'll want to smoke. I hate the smell.
Sheila: Your selfishness will make me weep.
Frederick: I think this flight is utter hell!

Traveling together is a severe test of affection or friendship, a fact which may justify some people in staying at home. The most strained relations result from one being knowledgeable and the other ignorant of the language. The better policy, therefore, is to avoid situations in which one's superiority over the other must become too obvious. Were they to decide on a visit to Labrador, Sheila and Frederick might at least begin on a level, neither knowing how to say "mush" to a dog team, even supposing that this would be the right thing to say.

To attempt to repeat the same holiday with the same friends is nearly always a mistake. Suppose that you and your husband agreed last year to meet Roger and Myra Flint at Dubrovnik. While there, at a splendid hotel in perfect weather, you unexpectedly met Barbara and Tony Steel, you and Barbara having been at school together. The Steels had already made friends with Helen Black, the novelist (recently divorced) and a stray bachelor called Timothy Butt.

There had followed some wonderful joint expeditions to

the interior, with dinner afterward on the terrace. The talk over the coffee was always stimulating and hilarious, the Flints and Steels always opposed in argument but the wives apt to change sides. Helen's knowledge of the country — to be the scene of her next book — added tremendous interest, and so did her slightly dangerous reputation. As for poor Timothy, he had been destined from birth to be ragged and seemed somehow to enjoy the role. Your husband, Michael, does not ordinarily pass as a wit but something in the situation made his talk seem incredibly funny; as when he used to insist that Timothy was the British Consul. When Timothy denied this, Michael would ask him why he had posed as Consul in the first place.

You, for your part, had been induced to sing and everyone had said afterward that you were marvelous. With no great pretensions ordinarily, you would seem indeed to have excelled yourself on the last night of your stay. When the party broke up, all swore to meet again next year at the same place and season. Christmas cards had been exchanged and there seems no reason why the holiday should not be repeated.

In point of fact, however, nothing of that magic quality is ever recaptured. You would do far better to go somewhere else, for the attempted repetition would go wrong and so spoil the memory of that earlier success. Back again at Dubrovnik, you would find that the Flints could not be there for the first week nor Helen for the last. Lacking the Flints, the Steels would turn out to be rather dull, without a spark of humor. Timothy, who promised at first to come, would cry off at the last moment — having fallen in love with a red-haired manicurist at the Sheraton Hotel off Park Lane — and Helen might be in a sulky mood when she finally appeared, her Yugoslav book having been badly reviewed. You would find yourself desperately trying to recapture a certain atmosphere of affection, gaiety and wit, and failing the more in that you would be trying too hard. On the last night together you would find that your voice had gone, the result of a cough. As for Michael, he would be sulky, to begin with, having wanted to visit Persepolis instead, and would finally show a tendency to flirt with Helen. His flirtation means nothing, of course, and there is little really to worry about, but you feel neglected. To teach him a lesson you might let Roger Flint kiss you, wishing afterward that you hadn't; and Myra's coldness toward you would add formality to the last farewell. The final promises to keep in touch would have been perfunctory in any case but the weather breaking so early would have been the finish. What bad luck, incidentally, that the only motion picture being shown should be a dubbed version of the Battleship Potemkin with the Odessa Steps Sequence spoiled by a break in the film!

Fairly anticipating all this, you will be wise to give Yugoslavia a miss for the time being. Explain rather, in terms of genuine grief, that Michael insists on seeing Persepolis. You need not add — but you inwardly know — that any attempt to reassemble the same party would be an almost certain failure. For "Never go back" is one of the golden rules.

Osborn

CHAPTER TWELVE

Retirement

THERE CAN BE no greater mistake than to suppose that we age rapidly after we retire. Legend would have it that we, the elderly, are deaf, blind, halt and lame, but nothing could be further from the truth. What we do find, to be sure, is that few people speak up as they used to do. Actors, for instance, have lost the art of delivering their lines so as to be heard even at the back of the house. We nowadays have to be in the front of the orchestra to hear anything. What must it be like in the balcony, where we used to sit in our young days? How odd that people should sit where they cannot possibly hear a word! As for our eyesight, that is just as good as ever it was, provided we have our spectacles. Our difficulty is when the spectacles are mislaid and we left without the means of seeing where they are. Smaller print is used these days, mind you, and other things have deteriorated, too. Even the simplest dish — like the ordinary boiled potato — lacks the taste it used to have; the result, no doubt, of all these chemical fertilizers.

But our energy has not suffered, far from it. We can walk further, thank heaven, than many of the younger folk we see around. As for our appearance, we have changed hardly at all. That is where our contemporaries have been less fortunate. Never shall we forget that Class Reunion Dinner at our old college, with people so decrepit as to be barely recognizable! We, by contrast, look and feel the same as we always did, full of vitality and young at heart.

It is among the ironies of life that we remain young behind the mask which others see. We are still faintly surprised when people already grown up address us with the respect due to age. We glance round to see whether someone more elderly is present, but there is no one as senior and we are thus made to realize that we are old. But what could be more absurd? We are as gay as ever, with an eye for the opposite sex and a capacity for mischief. We have never even conquered the shyness which held us back at the parties of (can it be?) fifty years ago.

There is nothing today so awe-inspiring, mind you, as the assemblies to which we were invited in those days. The host would be so distinguished, the hostess so brilliantly omnipresent, the dowagers so formidable and the ballroom so vast. You see nothing like it today. All we have now is old Susan and Robert, old Peter and Joan, people one was at school with, and nobody, surely, could be frightened of *them.*

This is how we reason with ourselves but with dwindling conviction. The face we see daily in the mirror has aged too gradually for us to see that we are no longer middle-aged. The last years have passed quickly and now, incredible as it may seem, we have reached the age of retirement.

The problem of superannuation is not the same for women as for men. For one thing, the man who retires may be actually older than his wife and may have developed some of the ailments which go with being elderly. For another, it is the man who retires, experiencing a shock to which his wife is not equally exposed. After going regularly to work for

Out
Tires

forty-five years, he suddenly finds himself free to do what he likes but unable, very often, to decide what it is he likes to do. His wife's routine is less affected, her problem arising merely from having him about the house at a time when she is used to sharing the place with her daily domestic help. Her immediate sensation is one of mild annoyance at finding him with the newspaper in the room she wants to dust and polish. Her choice lies between providing him with a workshop, studio or study, or else securing his election to the Town Planning Board.

It would be quite wrong, of course, to regard the whole system of local government as a device for keeping the retired executive out of the way of his wife's vacuum cleaner. The fact remains, however, that the abolition of all the local committees (following the appointment of a town manager) would cause widespread domestic crisis; a fact which political theorists would do well to keep in mind.

Where the previously active man goes completely out of circulation, failing to revive an old hobby or find a new interest, his wife will be faced with a serious problem, solved only when he dies (as he will) of boredom. She has to recognize that an able man without mortal disease, and not accident-prone, will live for about as long as he wants to live, surviving while there is something to hold his interest and dying, finally, because he has had enough.

The first secret of successful retirement is to phase out gradually, doing less work over the previous year or two and having some alternative occupation for the years which follow. Another secret lies in taking exercise without becoming a fanatic about it. While fishing and golf are to be encouraged, wives should normally restrain husbands who propose to sail singlehanded around the world. While occasional

heroes are acceptable, these ventures should remain more the exception than the rule. There are hazards enough in the passage round Cape Horn without adding the further risk of collision. Where exercise is concerned, enough is enough.

A third secret lies in avoiding the expression of vain regrets. We can look back on the poverty of our youth, bewailing the fact that we were denied then the more expensive meals we can now afford but cannot digest. We can dwell on lost opportunities for pleasure or romance or talk longingly of all the bargains we may have missed. For those who can recall the nineteen-thirties, and have since experienced the inflation of the nineteen-sixties, there is a bitter irony in recalling the things we could have bought while prices were as low as they once were. Had we foreseen the future we might have acquired property which is now worth millions. We could have picked up antique furniture, which has risen since in value by ten or twenty times the price we might once have paid. What would now cost $500 we might once have acquired for $25 or less, the sad fact being, however, that we did not possess $25 at the time when the opportunities offered. These are regrets upon which we should never dwell, not because they are depressing but because they involve a habit of looking back. When we cease to look forward, then we are old indeed.

The wife of a man who has retired should seek, first of all, to have interests other than in grandmaternity. She should not depend for her interests on a husband she will probably outlive. She should not depend for company upon children and grandchildren whose loyalty it is easy to overstrain. Her career, in its final phase, should be her own. She must avoid, however, the pitfalls which lie ahead, the obsessions, more especially, to which the old are liable. First of these is the obsession with one's ailments. Those with nothing better to do fall sick, settling down to a life of potions and pills. Most of the commonest complaints in later life are probably incurable, but everyone you meet knows of a remedy which did wonders for her first cousin or maiden aunt. Among the elderly the talk is thus apt to center upon herbal cures and sulfur baths, the magical properties of copper and the results to be expected from visiting this clinic or that. A sound rule is to ban all talk about ailments and avoid all reference to the problems of being overweight. The bathroom scales may be useful but they need not be dragged into calorie-conscious conversation. The truth is that various complaints cure themselves (at least temporarily) and that the periodic improvement we then attribute to whatever remedy we tried last. Our experience may not, therefore, be of value to anyone else. If there is a general treatment for illness it consists, plainly, in having other things to think about.

A second obsession to avoid is the one about carpets and furniture, china and plate. Our temptation in old age is to fuss endlessly about the inheritance of heirlooms. On the one hand, we may stand to inherit when our elder sister dies: on the other, we can talk forever about what we have to leave. If the portrait of Uncle Ebenezer goes to William, should Brenda have the display cabinet and Susan the writing desk? If the cutlery goes to Brenda, the fish knives might be more useful to William. Years can thus be wasted in dusting china and polishing silver which no one uses or will ever use, and relatives will bicker endlessly about why Nora should have the clock which great-aunt always said should go to Eve.

All these acrimonious discussions should die away on the

day when we come to move out, perhaps when the old home seems too big for just the two who are left. As the furniture comes into the full daylight, we suddenly realize that most of it is worthless. It was all right (wasn't it?) while it stood where it had always stood, but look now at the back! The carpets must have been threadbare for years but we never noticed. Those gray curtains, come to think of it, were originally green, and the lampshades, we suppose, must once have matched them. So gradual was the change that we thought everything as good as new. We had always believed in buying the best, mind you, and that rug in the living room is a case in point. That was purchased only the other day — well, a few years back — actually, in 1934 — and yet we can see now that it is (well, practically) worn out. It must have been of poorer quality than we realized at the time. In the open air we see that it is falling to pieces, not even worth cleaning and repair. Disputes about heirlooms are thus too often disputes about nothing.

If an obsession about furniture is to be avoided, there is still more reason to avoid being obsessed with a dog or cat, a parrot or canary. There are people whose later years are dogridden in a catastrophic way, some animal having all the status of a favorite son. When it is suggested that they escape the winter by a voyage to the West Indies, the whole scheme is made to hinge upon the welfare of the poodle. It cannot be considered if Fluff has to go to the ship's kennels. Would he be allowed to sleep in our cabin? No? Well, the rules are inconceivably barbarous! Why should the shipowners regard a small and harmless pet as a threat to the ship's safety? Do they think he will bite the helmsman at a moment of crisis? The idea is absurd. He never bit anyone except the postman, and that was only once and really the man's own fault, as he was afterward made to confess. If that is the regulation, however, there is nothing to be done about it. The sea or air passage is evidently out of the question, but the possibility remains of leaving Fluff with Cedric's cousin, Agatha.

"We did this once before but only for a weekend. To leave him for three weeks, however, is a different matter altogether. He might worry himself into an actual illness. There is also the problem of Agatha's cat. Now Fluff is the mildest and kindest of dogs, no one could deny that. He did once have a fight with a bull terrier but it wasn't his fault as even the terrier's owner had to admit. Fluff would hardly ever fight another dog but I must admit that he *does* chase cats. There is one that lives near us and gets chased up a tree every morning. That is a timid sort of creature but I daresay that Agatha's new Persian is ready to scratch a dog's eyes out. If Fluff were hurt, now, I should blame myself for going away. So Fluff cannot stay with Agatha.

"The only other plan I can think of is to place him with Grandmother at Martlesham. We tried this once and she was perfectly sweet about it, couldn't have been nicer. It was the year we went to Tangier and I'll never forget my parting with Fluff at Newhaven. Grannie came to fetch him — she lives near there — and I told Fluff that he must be on his very best behavior. The tears were in my eyes as we said goodbye, and so we set off for North Africa.

"I wish I could say I enjoyed the trip but the sad fact is that I could never forget Fluff's face as Grannie led him away. Each morning as we found ourselves having breakfast in Marseilles or Tunis or wherever it was, I could never forget the sorrowful look on my dog's face. We came to Algiers and our guide took us to visit the Casbah, the Arab quarter of the city where they sell curios and where that film was made with Hedy Lamarr and Charles Boyer. You have to be quite old, dear me, even to remember it. Well, we were sitting there in a café, drinking that strong coffee, and the guide was telling us what a dangerous place the Casbah used to be. He must have thought me terribly rude, for I suddenly said, 'How dreadful it must be for him to be without his mistress for all this time!' Our guide was called Osman and he had been telling us — as Cedric explained afterward — about one of the former Arab rulers, the Dey of Algiers. He thought it was the Dey I was talking about. "But he *wasn't* without his mistress. She was with him and so were his other wives, the whole harem, so it *wasn't* terrible for him." He was very solemn about it and I couldn't even *begin* to explain that it was my *dog* I was thinking about. He would never have understood — these natives never can — for you know how Arab dogs are treated — but Cedric and I laughed about it afterward, he talking of past history and I thinking only of my dog, the sort of thing no foreigner can make head or tail of.

"But it was at Gibraltar that I fairly broke down. I saw a dog there which looked exactly like Fluff! For a mad instant I thought that Fluff had followed us there like the collie in *Lassie Come Home*. Then Cedric pointed out that the dog we had seen was not really the same. He was not a poodle, to begin with, and he was much bigger and not black so much as brown and white with a shaggy coat and a curly tail. 'But the expression,' I cried, 'was exactly the same!' Cedric had seen only the stern of the dog and so knew nothing of its expression. All he could say was that it seemed to be different in breed, size, color and shape and I had to confess that he was right. I added firmly, however,

that I wanted to go straight home without the night we were to have spent in Paris. Fluff was pining away from grief and we had to rescue him at once! He went simply wild when we went to collect him. Grannie was a bit stuffy about it, I remember, saying that the dog had been perfectly well and better exercised than usual. She is too short-sighted, of course, to have seen the expression on his poor face. But I don't know whether I can ever leave him there again.

"I have heard people say that you can become too attached to a dog and some have even hinted that I am too obsessed with mine. I take no notice, of course, apart from deciding to have no more to do with them. There are people who would allow a dog to be vivisected or put down just because it has barked at the milkman. There are heartless and cruel people everywhere but we can at least avoid knowing them socially. Fluff means more to me, I'll admit, than half the folk I meet at a cocktail party. Cedric is almost as fond of him as I am, feeling as I do that Fluff is one of the family.

We don't often ask people in these days, in case Fluff should not like it. And holidays, as I have told you, can be difficult to arrange, with Fluff not liking to be left behind. I don't mind admitting that Cedric and I think the world of Fluff."

G. K. Chesterton once observed that a dog is splendid up to the point where you spell the word backward. There is less risk of obsession with a cat and there is most of all to learn from the cat in *Alice in Wonderland,* which had the trick of vanishing quite slowly, beginning with the end of the tail and ending with the grin, which remained some time after the rest of it had gone. "Well! I've often seen a cat without a grin" thought Alice, "but a grin without a cat! It's the most curious thing I ever saw in all my life." But is it so curious, after all? Is that not, rather, the proper way to go?